LEADING WITH EXECUTIVE PRESENCE

ANDY MATHESON

CONTENTS

INTRODUCTION 7
DEFINITIONS 9
THE FOUR QUADRANTS OF GRAVITAS 12
A BRIEF QUESTIONNAIRE 15

LEGEND 22
REPUTATION 23
POLITICAL AWARENESS 36
ACCOUNTABILITY 50

IMPACT 63
PROFESSIONAL IMAGE 64
SOCIAL SKILLS 86
INSPIRATIONAL PRESENTER 100

FOCUS 108
FUTURE ORIENTATION 109
CORPORATE VIEW 124
CLARITY 132

EGO STATE 155
PASSION 157
STATE MANAGEMENT 167
SELF-BELIEF 192

CONCLUSION 214

INTRODUCTION

Developing Executive Presence

In my business, I provide coaching support to senior managers and run workshops for those at the top of the organisation and those who aspire to be there. A host of skills and capabilities is necessary to be effective at this level, with one standout area of ambiguity. The term 'executive presence' is often mentioned, but few seem able to clarify what it means.

It is common for a member of the executive to give a direct report the feedback that they 'need to work on their presence', and to assume that the feedback has landed and is well understood. The person giving the feedback 'knows what it is when they see it', but the person on the receiving end may feel vague and uncertain about what it means and, indeed, what to do about it.

This book is the result of many years spent working with executives across many industry sectors. The Executive Presence Model on which this book is based was created with Ann Akers, who remains one of the very best leaders and executive coaches. Many of Ann's ideas and thoughts are summarised in these pages. Together, we have run many workshops on advanced coaching skills, executive presence and leadership, and I picked up the challenge of distilling all the learning and insights into this book.

In the coming pages, I aim to:

- o Bring clarity to the term 'executive presence'
- o Provide a model to help summarise and make sense of the territory
- o Provide a wealth of practical tips and ideas to help build presence at work

o   Make an authentic difference to the skills and behaviours of senior leaders at work

The Executive Presence Model on page 19 will provide you with an overview of the areas you may like to work on. From there, you can dip in and out of the relevant chapters. Each one is designed to explain and explore a different aspect of executive presence.

Definitions

Executive Presence – what is it and does it matter?

We need to bring some clarity to our definition of the term 'executive presence'. Let's explore each of these words individually and in combination.

'Executive' is a word associated with those at the most senior levels in an organisation. According to the Oxford English Dictionary, it is an adjective that means:

Relating to or having the power to put plans or actions into effect

The dictionary also gives an example of the word being used as a noun as follows:

A person with senior managerial responsibility in a business

'Presence' means the following:

The impressive manner or appearance of a person

In other words, presence is all about creating a positive impression in the minds of others.

These definitions help to provide a solid introduction, but research suggests we should tighten up the definition still further. Throughout this book we will be working with the following:

Executive Presence

A person who is perceived as credible and impressive at the most senior levels of an organisation

This definition is important, as it helps to frame the ideas and concepts within this book.

Firstly, I place executive presence into an organisation context. My concept of 'organisation' is all-embracing. I include within my research public, private and non-profit or charitable organisations. In terms of size, it doesn't matter whether you are the sole employee or one of over 10,000 people. Another key word here is 'senior'. My work focuses on those who need to help shape the future of the organisation. They also often need to be part of a team, making key decisions that have wide-reaching implications. In most cases, this will be the senior leadership team.

This definition also brings a clear focus on personal credibility and building an impressive reputation. In other words, I don't see executive presence as a cosmetic exercise. Certainly, looking and acting the part are important, but we also need people to be perceived as highly effective in their role. Some managers put on a suit and spout corporate BS at the meetings they attend – we have no time for pretentious charlatans. My definition and approach focuses on developing authentic credibility at board level.

This book will drill down to what it takes to build and develop executive presence at work. I will share many tools and techniques, and present you with various challenges and points for reflection. But first, let's begin with the four main quadrants that define our Executive Presence Model at the highest level.

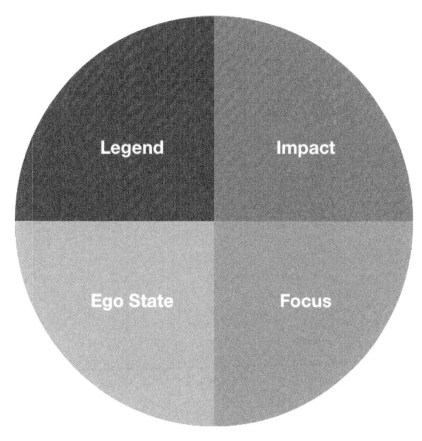

Fig 1 Executive Presence Quadrants

The Four Quadrants of Gravitas

What do people say about you when you are not there? You may not know the answer to this in full, but you can guarantee that people discuss you. The more senior you become, the more you are talked about. You may say, 'Well, I haven't really done much to talk about.' Rest assured, people will talk about that. Do you buy drinks at Christmas? Do you take the lead when no one else seems willing to do so? Do you stand up and challenge the traditionalists? Did you insult a colleague in a meeting recently? Did you keep quiet when perhaps you should have spoken up? Like it or not, gossip is part and parcel of corporate life.

What is your legend?

We all make quick assessments of people. In the blink of an eye, we make judgements about their background, their capability and their status. You have done this yourself whenever a candidate walks into a recruitment interview. Instantly, you make a snap decision about their suitability. You decide whether they are the sort of person you would like to work with ... or not.

Personal impact matters

Think for a moment about attending a senior leadership meeting. A typical meeting room with furniture designed to foster conversations; magnolia-coloured walls and carpets noticeable only by their lack of charisma (if, indeed, carpets have charisma). In other words, the layout, the function, the set-up of the meeting, whispers the word 'neutrality'.

Now imagine being a fly on the wall, eavesdropping on conversations. As you listen in, you notice a range of behaviours, and you realise that not all the participants in the meeting are equal. One of the participants talks forever. He loves the sound of his own voice, and wants to do nothing more than demonstrate his vast and extensive knowledge. The longer this goes on, the more you notice certain members around the table losing the will to live. Another team member seems defensive. She is asked about her team and their work on a new project. She launches into an attack on another department. Another seems worried about trivialities like car parking, staff parties, forms, processes and admin. You can't help but wonder why this seems to occupy so much of his time.

Only one person seems impressive. This person somehow has a finger on the pulse of the areas that really matter. She is able to direct the discussion to a few key areas, and doesn't allow overwhelming amounts of time to be devoted to operational trivia. This person has executive presence.

You are defined by where you focus your attention

It is time to tap into your emotions. Think about a time when you were last under extreme pressure. How did you behave? What would other people have noticed? Did you appear calm and in control, or would colleagues learn to keep out of your way? What was the tone of your language? Were you energetic, enthusiastic, optimistic? Or were you a doomsayer, spreading negativity and despondency to everyone you met?

More significantly, when you face your most difficult challenges, how do you feel? Are you confident, in control and powerful, or are you worried, panicking and weak?

We are defined by our levels of self-belief

Reflect on these questions, as they form the cornerstones of this book, and we will explore each in detail.

Legend: This quadrant concerns your reputation, your brand and how people talk about you in your absence. Everyone has some sort of reputation, and you have the potential to shape how you are perceived in the future.

Impact: This summarises how you come across to others. In this quadrant, we consider the first impressions you make when you enter a room, how you connect with people and your presentation skills.

Focus: Here we explore the focus of your energies and specifically how strategic you are in your approach to business. In this quadrant, we also look at how to clarify and simplify information.

Ego State: In the final quadrant, we explore self-belief and confidence in the role. Clearly, this is key to all the other parts of the model, and we will highlight these and many other links as we progress.

Within each quadrant we will drill down into more detail, as per the following diagram. You can see, for example, that 'Legend' contains sections on 'Reputation', 'Political awareness' and 'Accountability':

Legend	Impact	Focus	Ego State
Reputation	Professional image	Future orientation	Passion
Political awareness	Social skills	Corporate view	State management
Accountable	Inspirational presenter	Clarity	Self-belief

Fig 2 Executive Presence Structure

A brief questionnaire

On the next page, you will find a brief questionnaire. You might like to take a screen print of this, and tick the boxes next to the statements and comments that are the best fit for describing yourself. The questions cover all the key themes in this book, and will provide a starting point for an objective discussion around executive presence. Take your time, and make a note of any answers or comments you may wish to come back to later.

Key areas		High-level Definition	Is this me? Score yourself out of 10
Legend	Reputation	Positive - impressive - strong personal brand - a track record of success - high profile	
	Political awareness	Sensitive to other people's self-esteem - respectful - works around the hierarchy - understands the power systems	
	Accountability	Takes responsibility - prepared to challenge and deal with difficult issues - confronts 'the elephant in the room'	
Impact	Professional image	Smart - sharp - well groomed - organised - on time - well prepared - gravitas	
	Social skills	Empathy - listener - connects with people - interested - curious - networker	
	Inspirational presenter	Impressive - persuasive - interesting - engaging	
Focus	Future orientation	Thinks ahead - focuses on future business - shaping a new reality - talks strategy, customer, markets and change	
	Corporate view	Big picture thinking - whole company view - thinks about the wider implications of decisions	
	Clarity	Simplifies things - summarises - gets to the real issues - brings order to chaos - able to focus on priorities	
Ego State	Passion	Drive - enthusiasm - positivity - can do - radiates infectious energy - optimism	
	State management	Calm under pressure - unflappable - statesmanlike - respectful - emotional intelligence	
	Self-belief	Inner and outer confidence - resilience - positive self-talk	

Fig 3 Executive Presence Quick Questionnaire

Interpreting the results

As you can see, we have expanded the four quadrants of the Executive Presence Model by adding three subheadings to each area. This provides an essential level of detail that will help signpost the journey in this book, as well as help you think through your specific development needs.

Many people score this and ask, 'What does "good" look like?' I use this questionnaire in coaching sessions and on workshops, and my company collects data through our online versions of the questionnaire. Here are some trends I have discovered:

- Most people score themselves 6-7 out of 10. People seem comfortable with that.
- It is rare for anyone to volunteer a low score (4 or under). They don't like to be associated with the words that define low scores.
- Very few people score themselves 9-10. This feels perhaps egotistical, so many choose to respond more modestly.

This leaves 95% of people who complete this questionnaire falling into the 'Yes, I am generally okay, with a bit to learn and develop' category. In other words, **the raw data on the questionnaire is not reliable**. Do not use it to score yourself and put down your pen with a flourish and think, 'Great, I have nothing to worry about'.

There are a couple of sad truths you need to wrestle with when working on this topic:

1. Your self-perception may be wrong. There may well be some areas of development needed that you can't spot. Take the word 'clarity', for example. I doubt that your last memo, report or presentation was written to confuse people but perhaps it did. And indeed, many people intentionally write such reports.

2. Some of the areas on the model are quite sensitive and people worry about giving you honest feedback. It takes a brave and close friend to discuss your dress sense or your reputation in detail.

As you examine your results, you should accept that you probably have some work to do to improve your executive presence.

You may also like to talk through the questions with someone who knows you well and whose opinions you trust. The questionnaire truly comes to life when you are able to add observed perceptions to your own sense of self. So, find a close friend or colleague, take them for a coffee, wine or beer, and discuss the questionnaire in detail. Stress that you would really value some objective feedback. If you are feeling braver still, talk through the questionnaire and your responses with someone senior to you in your organisation whom you admire. The combination of self-disclosure and feedback with people you trust will provide you with a much more rounded view of how you come across.

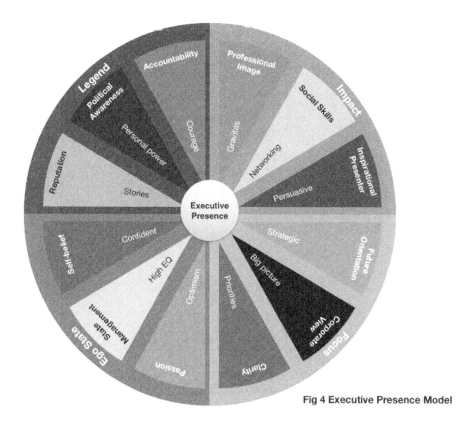

Fig 4 Executive Presence Model

This is the expanded Executive Presence Model that we will use to structure the remainder of the book. Let us be clear: it is not a perfect map of the territory. Models can rarely claim to be a perfect summary. However, I have worked with this model with many clients and have found it serves me well in raising awareness of the territory and enabling objective discussions around the subject.

There is no 'right' way to navigate through it. What works for me is to start in the 'Legend' section. I review a client's reputation, their understanding of the organisation's politics and power systems. I also review their sense of accountability, and challenge them to take responsibility for the obstacles they face.

I then work with the client and explore the areas that interest them, and where they feel they have the strongest development need. I suggest you do the same. By all means, read the book in order. The chapters start with 'Reputation' and end with 'Self-Belief', and that journey will make perfect sense. You will find, however, that each chapter stands alone. Feel free to cherry-pick your specific areas of interest.

Chapter summary

1. Our working definition of executive presence is: 'A person who is perceived as credible and impressive at the most senior levels of an organisation'.
2. Executive presence is about credibility and authenticity. It is not about 'show'.
3. The Executive Presence Model will enable an objective discussion around executive presence.
4. Many people fail to recognise their own development needs, and it is difficult to find people who will offer objective feedback.
5. Use the model to cherry-pick the relevant chapters from this book.

LEGEND

Building your Legend

This section deals specifically with the reputation you build over time, and what other people say about you. I have divided this into three main areas:

Reputation: A broad-brush view of the reputation you have crafted over time.

Political Awareness: The need to engage with the inevitable politics of organisational life.

Accountability: Your mindset when faced with challenges.

Reputation

If you work in and around an organisation, you will have developed a reputation. And, like it or not, you will continue to shape this reputation with every interaction. So, let's start with a few questions to get you thinking:

- What are you known for?

- What would an honest reference say about you?

- When people gather around the coffee machine and mention your name, what adjectives might they use?

- What stories would they tell?

- What is your biggest regret?

- What is your proudest achievement?

These questions all focus on your past, and therefore there is nothing that can be done about them. They also raise two interesting perspectives:

1. Your self-perception: your land of inner thoughts and how you evaluate your own life

2. Observations and conclusions made by others. You may have found the questions about other people's perceptions of you more challenging to answer, as it's impossible to know exactly what they think.

In order to make sense of the word 'reputation', we need to explore the origins of a reputation and track it back to its source. Here are a few examples:

- Heather would run to meetings. As she concluded one meeting, she would pick up her papers and run along the corridor, up the stairs and all the way to the next meeting room. People would hear her coming.

- Ian would join his team for a Christmas drink. He was the most senior person in the room and was a master at avoiding buying a round. He would always arrive ten minutes after everyone else to ensure that everyone already had a drink. He would then make sure his glass was just about empty when it was someone else's round.

- When Sean was on an off-site conference and it was time for bed, he would go to the bar and order two pints of bitter to take to his room.

- Justin was called for an interview and was asked to bring his portfolio. The interviewer asked to see a sample of his work, and Justin reached into a well-used shopping bag. He shuffled through some rather tatty documents until finally producing a selection of papers stapled together and handing them over.

These examples are all true. They have been chosen as examples here because they all concern real-life participants on training programmes or ex-colleagues (all names have been changed just in case they spot themselves). What they all illustrate is how reputations are formed in the briefest of moments. This is not by grand design – indeed, it is often the small, perhaps isolated incidents that are most noticeable, memorable and defining.

I apologise in advance for the following joke, but I think its inclusion here is necessary.

Four friends are sitting in a rural pub when a stranger walks in. After a while, they all get chatting and the stranger introduces himself. He turns to the first man, who says, 'Well, you will find my name goes back a long way. My father was a blacksmith, my father before him was a blacksmith and that's what I do now. And it will come as no surprise that I am Tom Blacksmith.'

Taking his cue, the second man introduces himself as Bill Cobbler. He goes on to explain the long history of his family's work with shoes.

The third man quickly joins in with his stories of tending the land and crop rotation across the generations. His name, of course, is Miles Farmer.

And so the stranger turns to the fourth man and says, 'How fascinating that professions stretching back a long way define who you are and what you are called. And you are?'

'Look,' said the fourth man, 'I only shagged one sheep.'

We begin to realise that reputations are often defined by singular moments. The moments when we are at our best, or indeed, our worst.

The other way to shape a reputation is to develop a pattern of behaviour that becomes noticeable over time. A simple example would be someone who is nearly always late for a meeting. It doesn't take long for this pattern to become picked up by others as a defining trait.

Shaping our reputation

There is little we can do to change our past. I remember chatting to an executive who started a long career in the organisation as a post boy, before working his way up to senior leadership. He complained that some of the senior leadership team (who pre-dated his arrival) still had a strong memory of him in that job, and he struggled to get past that. In that case, there are times when the only way to reshape a reputation is to move on. However, for most people there is a chance to remould perception. Here are some of the key areas I explore with my coaching clients:

1) Legend building

There is a famous quote by the American philosopher and psychologist, William James (1842-1910), that reads as follows:

'The greatest discovery of any generation is that a human being can alter his life by altering his attitude.'

This quotation challenges the whole concept of a 'reputation', and suggests that people are perfectly capable of changing their life by a shift in mindset. So let us use this concept to explore how it is possible to shape a reputation, rather than be defined by one.

Imagine that you have an important presentation in two weeks' time; a lot is riding on the outcome and you need to perform to your best. Consider for a moment the preparation you might do for such a presentation. When I ask this question to coaching clients, they reel off a number of predictable things to think through and work on in advance. Checking the room, reviewing the purpose of the presentation, thinking through the needs of the audience and developing a slide deck are all common areas of preparation. There is, however, a common trend in how people respond to the preparation question. They tend to focus on things/people other than themselves, and they think about the lead up to the presentation rather than the impact they will make at the end.

The following four questions can help shift focus and adjust preparation. If done well, this can prove transformational in terms of impact and reputation. The word 'presentation' here can be replaced by 'interview', 'meeting', 'networking' or other event as required.

1) **At the end of your presentation, what do you want people to think?**

This question gets to the root of the impact you want to make on a client or colleague's thoughts. We often want to shift people intellectually. For example, we want a reluctant client to think maybe they will buy from you. Perhaps you are hoping a frugal finance director will look more kindly at your project proposals. Perhaps you are looking for an intellectual endorsement of your value, contribution or worth. Whatever it is you wish to see in terms of mental shift, write it down.

2) **At the end of your presentation, what do you want people to feel?**

This question is important as it addresses the emotional impact you have on others. When you reflect on other presentations you have attended, the best ones have energised you, made you feel alive, perhaps challenged or upset you. The worst have bored you, annoyed you or even caused you to question your sanity. In other words, you can look back on a history of emotional reactions to every interaction. Think about the last time you watched a movie: the best films connect with you on an emotional level. Great leaders realise that working life operates on the same level. So, write down the words that you want to leave people feeling. If you want them to feel confident, proud, excited, loved, energised, determined or important, write it down.

3) **At the end of the presentation, what do you want people to say to you as you wrap things up? Or to each other after you have left the room?**

People always talk about their experiences, so what words would you like to hear hanging in the air? I recall working with a compliance officer who was trying to get the board to appreciate the need to tighten up company policies and procedures. When I asked him what he would like them to say at the end, his reply was perhaps less corporate than I was expecting. 'Thank God you are here' was what he wanted. He knew his job wasn't the most popular in the company, but he also knew he could save them money and preserve their reputation by bringing some important issues to the table. He needed to hear recognition that he was valued. When you think through this question, please write down the words and phrases you would like people to actually use.

4) **At the end of the presentation, what do you want people to do?**

Again, a critical question that gets to the heart of why you are doing what you are doing. For some events, this is easy to fathom. The salesperson will often expect a phone call confirming an order, or an applicant will want a job offer. But how about an off-site management conference? What do you want people to do as a result of that? Surely people just turning up isn't enough. You need to be clear on your call to action. So, think this through and write down some specifics.

The four questions above work just as well for arranging a dinner party as they do for presenting to senior leaders in the boardroom. Think of an upcoming event that is important to you. It can be anything of significance, either at work or at home. Take a single piece of paper, write the heading on the top and then write out your responses to these questions in full. Then take a good look at what you have written. I believe this process can have a huge impact on you and what you wish to achieve. Here's why it works:

By thinking through the impact you want to make, you become more aware of the deeper goals of what you are doing and why. In this example, a presentation is not an end in itself. People will not be simply ticking a box that says, 'Yes, the presentation was completed' or, 'Yes, I attended the management meeting'. Those present will have an emotional reaction to you, and they will take action based on their experience. So you need to manage and prepare for that.

By thinking these things through, your preparation moves up to a new and improved level. I was working with a manager who was preparing for a company off-site and I asked him what he wanted people to feel as a result of attending. He wrote down the words 'valued', 'important', 'consulted' and 'loved'. He then reviewed the plan for the off-site meeting and noticed full days of presentations, updates and slides with almost zero interaction. There was no space for praise, no time for consultation and certainly no sign of love. The questions prompted him to make some big changes to the agenda and tone of the meeting.

There is a strong customer orientation hidden beneath the questions. Although they seem to be focussed on you, they force you to get inside the head of those on the receiving end of you and the impact you will make.

By starting to think this through and preparing yourself to manage the impact you will have, there will inevitably be a shift in how you come across to people. For example, if you are going to a sales meeting and want to come across as 'warm', you will find yourself going into the meeting with a heightened awareness of the need to be more connected than usual. You will find that, by processing and thinking through the impact you wish to make, your actions and behaviours are far more likely to produce the outcome you seek.

I call the technique 'Legend Building' and find it to be an incredibly valuable coaching tool. I have noticed that it can help in two ways. Firstly, in the example above, the questions are asked well in advance as an aid for preparing on many levels. The second way it can be used is just before a meeting or any important event.

In our consultancy roles, my colleagues and I often find ourselves in reception areas and coffee shops, waiting for meetings to start. As part of our preparation, we have now taken to asking each other these questions just before we go to meet our clients. It reminds us of the impact we wish to make and the way we want to behave. We might use words like 'respectful of their expertise' or, 'great listeners' or, 'fun to work with'. We know that by bringing these words out into the open, we begin to shape our behaviour in the meetings. Without them, we have been guilty of filling meeting time with too much information and too many slides and perspectives.

Before we leave this topic, there is one other use for the approach that you may find helpful. All the examples above are personal and reflect one person's impact and preparation. You can also use these four questions from a team point of view, and they work particularly well when trying to build a 'legend' or reputation at senior leadership level. Next time you have a leadership team meeting, perhaps you can reflect on these questions by pointing them at the impact the senior leadership team will have on an organisation. The impact will be significantly wider and be about larger numbers of people, but they are still pertinent questions. What do you want your people to think, feel, say and do as a result of your leadership?

2) Managing social media presence

Many readers will be active on social media, which creates both opportunities and threats for those aiming to make a positive impression. There have been several famous cases where people have come to regret things they have posted online later in their career. We can all recall politicians whose extreme views have come back to haunt them. Only this morning I read a national newspaper article about a chief executive who has been uncovered as big game hunter. The picture of him sitting proudly next to dead animals with a gun by his side has done little for his own or his organisation's PR. The story was broken when a smart journalist linked a personal Instagram account to the organisation profile.

So, what should your attitude be towards social media postings? Here are a few dos and don'ts:

- Most readers will have a LinkedIn profile. Make sure you have a professional-looking picture on there. Don't have a dodgy photo from a drunken night out, no matter how it amuses you. You may love your kids, but don't put pictures of them instead of you or with you as your profile picture.

- Make sure your career summary and personal statements are up-to-date and well written. Don't allow poor grammar and bad spelling to creep into your profile.

- Some people are very active on LinkedIn. Others are less so. Whatever your strategy, make sure you manage your connections and your networking carefully.

- A lot of people ask for comments on social media. They write things like, 'I would love your views on this.' They rarely mean this. What they are really saying is, 'I am posting this as I want a bit of personal PR, so please tell me you like it.' By all means support the things you like, there is nothing wrong with that. My advice is to remember that there is a time and place for criticism and feedback, and public social media postings are rarely a good idea. If you have strong opinions, write a personal note.

- If you can, separate out the personal and professional connections on social media. I know this is hard, as some colleagues cross over from business and become friends.

Many people use sites like Facebook and Instagram for social reasons. Whether you merge personal and professional life online is up to you, but do bear in mind that your private life then becomes visible to your colleagues. So the drunken night out, fancy dress costumes and fixation with cat videos all begin to shape your reputation.

One of the joys of social media is the opportunity to be exposed to other people's views, preferences and thoughts. There is a danger in this, however. Some posts use controversial humour to make a point. Often highly charged political views begin to circulate. Be especially aware of adding a 'share' or a 'like' to things that may be perceived by others to be homophobic, discriminatory or libellous. Social media tends to have an amazing memory, and the quick likes and shares can come back to haunt you.

3) We are defined by stories

You will be aware of the power of stories and how this impacts a reputation. Customer service legends can rise and fall on the back of a well-told story, just as a business can suffer when things go publicly wrong. I expect you have several personal stories to tell that have shaped your perception of an organisation following your own customer service experiences.

The same is true of senior leaders. Take a moment to think about some of the managers and leaders you have worked for over the years and then mentally line them up on a scale of one to ten, where ten is the best and one is the worst. I am guessing you have maybe one or two at the extremes and a bunch of people around the middle in a classic bell curve shape.

I would love to explore the traits and characteristics of the very best people on your list, but the written word doesn't facilitate that (although by all means drop me an email). Here are some predictions:

- The best leaders get a lot of small things right. They are probably not perfect, but spend time with them and they will work hard to connect and engage with you on a personal level.
- You will remember the time they came to you with a problem and said the magic words, 'What do you think?'. They didn't pretend they knew everything and they were genuinely interested in your opinion.
- You will remember a meeting that was actually fun and engaging. The leaders did something to spice it up and make it memorable.
- You can point to a number of occasions when they have stood up and praised you and the wider team, rather than take personal credit for success.
- You can remember when they accepted responsibility for a problem when it was clear the source was from within the team.
- When you reflect on your own development and learning journey, you can recall moments when they have been by your side, coaching, mentoring and challenging you. You know that you are in a better place today than you were a year ago as a direct consequence of their support.
- They remembered the small things in your life. They asked about the family, your team, your weekend, birthdays and even the dog.
- They bought the coffee, went to the bar and tidied up at the end of the day. They didn't rely on 'junior' people to do the more mundane tasks.
- They used handwriting and handshakes as commonly as other people use emails. They worked out that time in people's company can be transformative in relationship building.

- When you think of them, you picture someone smiling, not complaining.
- When the pressure is on, they roll up their sleeves and set an example.
- They are kind and compassionate, and you can identify a number of moments when they have clearly thought about the people rather than the profits, results or numbers.
- They tell the truth when others might avoid it, and you can remember the respect in the room generated by these moments of honesty.

The list could of course be longer, and I am sure you will have your own versions of these points. This leaves a question for you to ponder. What stories are you creating? What do people say about you when you are not there?

Chapter Summary

We shape our reputation over time. The more senior you are, the more visible your deeds and actions.

1. People notice what you do and what you don't do.
2. You can shape a reputation by thinking about the outcomes of key interactions. We call this 'legend building', and this technique can be widely used to help strengthen your credibility.
3. Every day contains limitless opportunities for you to create a positive, credible and lasting impression. Take a moment to think what you might do to today to shape your reputation.

Political Awareness

The nature of power and politics is often complex. Many clients will use expressions such as, 'He is a very political animal' or, 'This feels like a political organization.' To simplify this, we will explore a number of key issues in this chapter:

- What we mean by power, where this comes from and what difference this makes
- Using your personal power to get things done
- Visible signs of power and what to do about it
- Abuse of power
- #MeToo
- The power of authentic challenge
- Navigating impossible people

Power, influence and structure charts

What gives you the right to hold any influence over the people around you? What is the source of your power? Many people are simply given 'stripes' on their shoulders. They have a job title like 'Head of' or 'Vice President' or 'Director', and they can point to a structure chart that shows their role in relation to others'. The chart contains nice neat boxes, and the arrangement of work and responsibility all seems clear. Quite often, an organisation will write detailed job descriptions and invest in even more detailed competency frameworks so that all roles are clear and can be explained and accounted for. I remember seeing such a framework for a famous car manufacturer, amounting to nearly three metres of paperwork that detailed every role, every reporting line and every key responsibility. If you needed to understand any role in the structure, you could simply look it up and there it was, in black and white.

Naturally, this all makes perfect sense until someone in the role looks at their profile and concludes that it bears no resemblance to real life. The reality of any organisation is a mass of connections, many tangled lines that ebb and flow as time passes. Nothing is static and nothing is that clear. Project teams cross over functional lines, departmental structures become vague, and accountabilities and responsibilities are much more random.

So in the middle of this complexity, what are the sources of power and influence?

Stripes and formal authority: Some roles do carry official sign-off responsibility. There are often budget limits on roles or authorisation levels that enable decision-making at certain levels in an organisation. In addition, some roles carry benefits like car parking spaces, window spaces, desk size and plant allocation. I remember with some amusement that one of my early roles entitled me to a plant in a pot and a space by the window. I was also senior enough to have a secretary, and I was allowed to approve time off and sign off some invoices and performance management scores.

Knowledge and expertise: It is often said that 'knowledge is power', and in organisational life, there is a truth to this. People with a long history of service can provide an essential perspective on current problems. A company lawyer will suddenly find themselves in the centre of power when new contract negotiations come to the fore. It is not good enough to simply have a job title to gain this sort of power. You need authentic expertise that you have demonstrated can add value.

Charisma: Some people develop a range of skills and confidence that can inspire people. They are able to carry a compelling and powerful message that can sway an audience or capture the hearts and minds of an individual.

Informal authority: Some individuals have, on paper at least, little formal authority in their organisation, but spend time in their company and you will observe significant power and influence. An obvious example is a PA to a member of the executive team. The connection they can develop with the senior leader can evolve way beyond the terms of the job description. They can become confidante and friend, and advise on a myriad of issues. More importantly, they can be a gatekeeper for their boss and decide who has access. I also remember a training organisation with a large network of associates. In the middle of the organisation was a lady called Jenny, who exerted a significant influence over who was allocated the work. Anyone who wanted to be put forward for any work had to get Jenny on side.

Bully: I am not comfortable writing this one, but I do accept the reality of this source. Some people are bullish, aggressive and domineering, and can create waves in an organisation by the sheer force of their personality and their tone. I recall a leader from early in my career who struck fear into most people in the office. He had a legendary temper combined with a willingness to cut people down to size with quips and insults.

Enthusiasm: This may seem a strange item to put down on our list of sources, but energy and enthusiasm do carry weight. Recently, I was at a meeting where a collection of equals gathered to discuss networking opportunities. At the end of the meeting, one person volunteered to pick up the actions, summarise the outcomes and draft a proposal. Of course, everyone agreed to their suggestion but in that moment, a power shift occurred. Suddenly, one person became more significant in terms of progress and movement. It doesn't matter whether you are the first to suggest something or, indeed, the first to follow an idea. There is power in your energy and commitment.

Chairman-like behaviour: When Dr Meredith Belbin conducted his research into the successful make up of teams, he noticed a number of roles that had influence over the group. He described the role of coordinator and used the symbol of an orchestra conductor to summarise them. This research ties in well to our review of sources of power. If a group of colleagues is working a problem, there is significant power in the person who clarifies the goals and objectives, who checks in on progress towards these, who summarises the feelings and ideas from the team, and who invites contribution from others. In a way, this is the opposite of the concept of power through knowledge. Indeed, Belbin defines the coordinator as having an allowable weakness of not necessarily being the most clever or knowledgeable person in a team. Instead, such power comes from goal setting, summarising and facilitation.

Praise, thank yous and favours: One of the best business books I have read is Robert Cialdini's Influence: The Psychology of Persuasion. He describes a fascinating case study about how a waiter can improve the amount of a tip they get. It seems we are swayed by the delivery of a mint or small chocolate to accompany the bill. This small gesture inspires us to feel beholden to the waiter and to offer a tip for their services. Clearly, there is a connection between some of the informal gestures we make and the level of loyalty they inspire.

When you reflect on this list, it is interesting to note that only one of the sources is really about the power that formal authority provides. It becomes apparent that appointment to a role that carries a level of authority is only powerful to a degree. There are clear limitations in relying on authority to get things done, and I would suggest the following as essential tips for raising your own levels of power and influence:

- ○ Personal development. If knowledge is power, then investing in your own development is a no-brainer. Whatever your profession, you need to keep yourself up to date within your field of expertise and from a wider perspective. Be hungry for new thinking, new ideas and developments, and changes to your industry and markets.

o Become a master presenter. Our chapter on presentation skills is a mere starting point here, but you need to master the art of being compelling on your feet. Many influencing techniques can be learned.

o Develop and improve your own skills as a coach/facilitator. They are more powerful than perhaps you realise.

o Work out who is really important in the organisation and connect with them (more on this later).

o Build on your skills in setting goals and searching for areas of agreement. Become an ace summariser – bringing clarity to confusion is a key executive skill (again, more on this later).

o Use your energy and enthusiasm to get to the heart of the action.

o Do favours for people, be generous with your time and attention, and couple this with praise and recognition for others.

Using personal power to get things done

In my role, I am fortunate to walk into many organisations and to meet many people. I have listened to countless complaints about the frustration of not achieving goals. It is apparent there are many barriers between ambition and reality. It is not easy to make rapid and impressive progress. There also appear to be many organisational 'hangers on'. People who grasp the coat-tails of the business and attend meetings, and send and reply to emails without adding much value for the time they spend on all this.

I would like to suggest that executive presence requires a re-evaluation of use of personal power, and to challenge all readers to think about the following questions:

o Are you surrounded by impressive people?

- ○ Is there potential for the results of your team to improve?
- ○ What influencing strategies do you currently use to get things moving?
- ○ How tolerant are you of inaction and excuses?
- ○ Are you able to practise ruthless compassion?
- ○ Are you the spider in the middle of the web?

Developing connections

I was recently sitting in the reception of a large corporate organisation, and was struck by the huge number of people entering the building, swiping through the barriers and disappearing into the labyrinth of corridors and rooms. I was reminded of a lecture I attended by Professor McDonald at Cranfield University many years ago. He asked what appeared to be a rather random question: 'How many people do you love in your life?' He then invited people to provide suggestions. Inevitably, we heard contributions about husbands, wives, partners, children and parents. Then he asked for the number of close friends and acquaintances, and again we responded with drinking buddies, neighbours, members of clubs and societies. Professor McDonald's presentation was about marketing strategy and, specifically, key account management. He wanted to alert people to the reality of forming close customer connections and the severe limitations of spreading a sales representative too thinly by covering an area that is too large.

Years later, as I sat in that reception area, his comments resonated with the vast numbers of people entering the building and the reality of developing meaningful relationships and connections. You will never know everyone; you will never connect with everyone. In practise, you have to make choices about how to spend your networking time and the connections you forge.

I don't want to get too scientific here, but I feel a two-by-two matrix coming on (Professor McDonald would be delighted)...

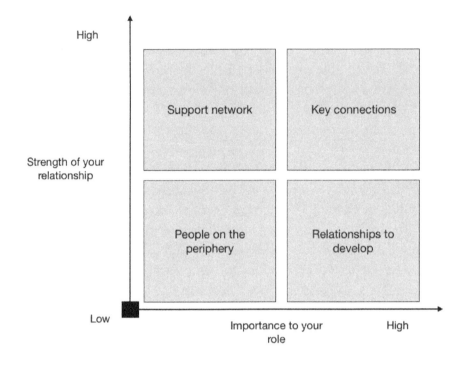

High

Strength of your
relationship

Low

| Support network | Key connections |
| People on the periphery | Relationships to develop |

Importance to your
role

High

Fig 5 Networking Matrix

There will always be people on the periphery of your radar: people you recognise, but don't know. Equally, you will have some close friends and connections at work who are not really connected to the work you do. For example, you may know someone who you used to work with, but your career paths have moved in different directions.

The key box in this matrix for the topic of power is the 'Relationships to develop' box. This recognises there are people in the organisation who are key to your success, and yet you have only a distant connection with them. This is not a description of hierarchical levels. The people here can be from any level and any part of the organisation, and you should consider identifying them and doing something to strengthen your connection to them. There is no magic formula for purposeful networking, but try these:

Own it: The people who are important to you are unlikely to wake up and think of the need to connect with you. So it is up to you to take the initiative.

Coffee with questions: Drop someone an email that simply suggests you meet for an informal chat, as you would love to hear more about things from their perspective.

Advice: As in, ask for it. The one question that will generate a response from anyone is, 'I could do with some advice.'

Invitations: If you are holding a team meeting or an off-site, invite people to join you. Don't make them sit through hours of turgid discussions, or force them into a regular commitment. Focussed invites on specific topics will help forge connections.

Listen: Great networkers realise the key to success is to find out about other people, not to tell them about themselves.

Thanks: There is considerable power and respect in a statement like, 'Before I present our research findings, I would like to thank Sarah and her team for providing their fresh perspectives.' People like to hear recognition for their advice and contributions.

Use RACI as part of your project planning. This stands for Responsible, Accountable, Consulted and Informed, and is a reminder of the different roles in managing a project. Being clear on who is responsible for project is important, and you also need to be clear on who is ultimately accountable. The questions around who to consult and who to inform about progress are also key and in response to these, you will identify the people across the organisation with whom you need to connect.

Visible signs of power

I have a thing about people who proclaim themselves to be something when they are not. I have often seen a poster on an office wall with the words, 'You don't need to be mad to work here, but it helps.' Only the dullest of people put that poster up! The neighbour who wears a T-shirt bearing the words 'Party Animal' is anything but. The person who proudly declares themselves as funny and outrageous is often perceived as neither. I suppose I believe the evidence of style, behaviour and impact far more than the proclamation.

In a way, this whole book is about authentic power and credibility. The best leaders I know ooze class and credibility, even when away from their office and their over-sized executive chair. There are, however, a few realities to deal with here. The more senior you are, the more you get paid. Your car may be bigger, your office larger, your department more expansive. You may be on a different floor on the building. You may have better furniture, a better view and your own meeting area. I am not going to suggest you shouldn't enjoy these things. But you need to be careful about how you use the trappings of status and the signals you send to others.

Don't allow your status to become a barrier to connecting with people. If you have your own office, make sure you have plenty of meetings in an open-plan space. Encourage people to use your space when they need it. Make people feel comfortable when they meet you. Warmth and genuine respect go a long way. It may sound trivial, but the layout of seating and how you meet and greet people says a lot about you. Your juniors can feel intimidated by levels of seniority, so beware of sitting in a dominant leather chair, looking down on those you survey like an organisational lord of the manor.

Abuse of power

Some people seem to love demonstrating power by being critical of others, especially in public. They use tactics like humiliation and dismissive gestures to get people to bow to their views and ideas – tactics that begin to define them and can become the stuff of legends. We have all seen army movies where the new recruit is subject to humiliation at the hands of an authoritarian drill instructor. Some managers adopt this behaviour as something to role model. In my view, there is no place for this in an organisation. Don't get me wrong, we can still provide tough challenges to individuals and teams, but not with such authoritarian flourish.

The implications of this behaviour are worrying for organisational health and culture. People learn that the best ways to stand up to a bully are either avoidance or agreement. So they will give you a wide berth if they can, or will sit in a meeting, nodding sagely, as if hanging on every word. Then they will moan at the coffee machine and gossip about the poor quality of leadership. Over time, whole teams and departments can shrink into themselves and adopt a culture where avoidance of harm and not rocking the corporate boat become prevalent.

I often mention to attendees on our development programmes that leaders get the staff they deserve. The organisational bully will develop a negative and unpleasant environment. The comparison I would like to remind you of is parents watching their kids participate in competitive sports on the school playing field. There are few things less classy than the parents who shout abuse at the referee, are visibly exasperated by every decision made and who call out errors with aggression. Even worse are the parents who are especially condemning of the effort made by their own children. It seems that these same parents then come to work and apply the same behaviour to the people in their team. Not only is this counterproductive on every level, but it quickly builds a reputation of someone who is not in control of themselves or others.

#MeToo

While I have been writing this, there has been considerable media coverage of the #MeToo movement. A case against a heavyweight Hollywood mogul is still live. The music business is equally rife with accusations of abuse of power and sexual manipulation. And only today I read of a CEO who has resigned amid rumours of inappropriate behaviour.

These reports all serve as a reminder that reputations are only as strong as the worst moment in a career. It goes without saying: There is no place for sexual misconduct in the workplace. Over the last decade, I have worked with many organisations and am delighted to have witnessed progress in areas such as diversity, inclusion and equality. Yet I am troubled to still find patronising or inappropriate behaviour in some organisations. I can't legislate against it, but in a book about executive presence, I can at least provide some clear statements of support to the #MeToo movement.

Here are my thoughts on the personal values that should live with you:
- o I am rarely the smartest person in the room.
- o I am surrounded by people with huge potential, alternative perspectives and original ideas.
- o I believe in strength through diversity.
- o I believe in equality and I treat everyone with respect.
- o Positive thoughts and energy come from everyone, albeit in different ways, but all forms have power and value. True leaders recognise and nurture this.
- o I need divergent thinking, not acolytes. Cognitive diversity encourages innovation and provides opportunities to avoid group think and suboptimal decision making.

- I won't tolerate inappropriate behaviour and will call people out when I see it. I encourage others to not be bystanders.
- I have zero tolerance for sexual innuendo and stereotyping in the workplace.
- I will champion inclusivity and fairness.
- I will implement terms and conditions that are fair and accessible to all, and that do not directly or indirectly discriminate against anyone.
- I will be a powerful role model and ally for all my people, regardless of protected characteristics.

Whilst most leaders will nod sagely to the above list of values, it is worth reminding you that this is a book about building authentic leadership and credibility at the most senior levels. There have been great strides forward in the areas of diversity and equality over the last couple of decades, but there is clearly more to be done. In terms of executive presence, inclusive leadership as a competency and skillset is and will continue to be a key differentiator for the highest performing senior leaders.

Authentic challenge

Earlier in the chapter, I mentioned there is no place for bullying. But there is certainly a place for feedback and challenge. Your role is to raise the bar on performance and that means being prepared to have some difficult conversations. Real power comes from your intent. Which of these two statements resonates with you?

1. I believe in your potential. I am prepared to coach and develop you, and sometimes I may share some challenging thoughts and feedback with you to help you.
2. I love demonstrating my power and superior expertise. I will regularly and publicly tell you how bad you are to remind you of my own superiority over you. Perhaps you

will take heed of some of my pearls of wisdom to make your own life slightly less miserable.

Okay, so maybe I worded the questions to make response Number 1 a no-brainer. But there is an important core assumption to the power question. Using personal power wisely is all about intent, and a key consideration is – who benefits from your use of power?

In my view, you build credibility through being prepared to ask challenging questions that will bring different thinking to a room full of people nodding in agreement. Or, you build credibility by being prepared to offer feedback to someone who could be even better with development.

Navigating impossible people

Most organisations have people in senior roles who are difficult to deal with. These people are often good at managing upwards or have the ear of an even more senior member of staff. In some cases, their length of service and expertise provides them with a commanding role in an organisation. Naturally, there is no magic formula for dealing with these people, but perhaps a few common sense reminders will help.

- o   Work with them, not against them.
- o   Ask for help and advice rather than tackle them head on.
- o   If they do something you don't agree with, remain calm, explain your dilemma and ask for their perspective on how to solve it.
- o   Consult with them more than you need to.
- o   Invite them to your team meetings.
- o   Support them in public.
- o   Be open and honest with them, but keep disagreements for your one-to-one meetings. Don't take them on in public.

Chapter Summary

1. Organisations are complex and political, and you need to spend time thinking through how they work in reality, not just on paper.
2. Master political awareness rather than becoming a master of politics.
3. Manage power wisely and with a focus on getting things done, but not at the expense of others. Balance use of power with strong emotional intelligence.
4. There is no place for abuse of power or discrimination.
5. Authentic power comes from gaining the trust and respect of others.

Accountability

There is a famous allegory that goes as follows:

This is a story about four people named Everybody, Somebody, Anybody and Nobody. There was an important job to be done and Everybody was sure that Somebody would do it. Anybody could have done it, but Nobody did it. Somebody got angry about that, because it was Everybody's job. Everybody thought that Anybody could do it, but Nobody realised that Everybody wouldn't do it. It ended up that Everybody blamed Somebody when Nobody did what Anybody could have done.

In my travels, I have seen many instances where this seems a neat summary of organisation culture and raises the key issue of accountability. This may be a small chapter in this book, but it has considerable significance on executive credibility and on getting things done.

To explore this, we will look at three main areas in this section:

1. Yes, it is your crisp packet

2. How do you build a climate of accountability in your team?

3. Guiding principles for accountability

Yes, it is your crisp packet

Let us firstly have a look at the crisp packet. At the World Cup in 2018, much was written about the football matches, but the fans also received considerable press coverage. One such reported case was the Japanese fans who became famous for the way they cleaned up the stadium. They were filmed at the end of the game going along the seats with bin liners, making sure they had picked up all the rubbish around them.

The world is full of people who are waiting for other people to do things to make things better. Listen to a radio interview on local community problems and you will hear many calls for 'the government' to sort things out. Go to a meeting and you will hear calls for 'the company' or 'the management' (whoever they are) to do something. Even at individual level, you hear people blaming others for issues clearly within their control. I was most amused chatting about weight loss to a friend who blamed her partner for leaving chocolate bars around the house for her lack of progress on a diet.

One of the diagrams that carries a lot of weight for me is the accountability ladder. I confess to not designing this, and many different versions can be found in the business world, but it is without doubt one of the most useful coaching and leader development tools.

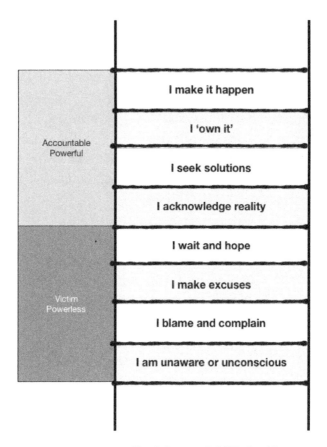

Fig 6 Accountability Ladder

As you can see, the ladder has a number of levels.

I am unaware or unconscious: This level is specifically aimed at the mindless and the unenthusiastic, who will use expressions like, 'Don't ask me, I only work here.' If you sit on this rung, you have no interest in anything around you, and you feel completely disconnected from the goals of the business or the nature of the problem.

I blame and complain: If you sit on this rung, you love to complain about things, especially the inaction of other people.

You see problems as other people's fault and you can spend many hours directing negative energy at them. It doesn't get anything done; it makes you miserable to be around, although perhaps letting off steam is therapeutic in some way.

I make excuses: As part of my role in developing and coaching professionals, I find myself marking assignments, and am often amused by the excuses that arrive as students approach deadline day. Sadly, electronic communication has ruined the 'dog ate my homework' excuse, but this has been replaced by corrupt hard drives, dead grandmas, ill children and miscellaneous work pressures.

I wait and hope: People sitting on this rung believe that things may work out in the end and all they need to do is be optimistic, observant and patient. This can be coloured by a deep-seated concern that they may well be disappointed.

These first four rungs all have something in common: they are grouped by the words 'victim' and 'powerless', and all carry the assumption that someone else needs to do something to fix the problem. In coaching and leader development, we see it as a primary focus to get people off these rungs of the ladder.

The upper four rungs are where we need people to be, so let's have a look at them.

I acknowledge reality: Sometimes people need to face tough situations and see them as they are. For example, a classic complaint brought to coaching is 'my boss is an idiot'. Well, that may be true (it sometimes is), but poor leaders have a habit of managing upwards well. So the hard reality is that the boss, even if they are as idiotic as described, is probably good for another couple of years in post at least. This means our client needs to face up to dealing with a poor-quality leadership. There is no point sugarcoating reality.

I seek solutions: Once you have ownership, the next step is to work the problem and resolve it. Sometimes there is no solution, in which case you have to decide to stop complaining and just get on with it.

I 'own it': This is where our Japanese football fans shine. They have a mindset that says, we created the mess, or at least some of it, so let's get on with cleaning it up. Being an impressive leader means taking ownership of the issues and problems. Your mindset is one of power and responsibility and probably assuming that no one else will do anything.

I make it happen: Here you drive the change necessary in yourself, your team or your connections. You don't seek permission to do this – again, you just get on with it.

Let's explore this avenue further.

I was working with a senior team in London, and the CEO had handed out a challenge concerning innovation and excellence. The organisation had adopted a new value of excellence, and each team was charged with developing plans and actions to bring this to life. The team in front of me had made no progress and when I asked them why, they explained they were still awaiting guidelines on the definition of excellence to which they should aspire.

This one case is symptomatic of the mindset of many teams I encounter. Whole teams of people sit around wondering when 'head office' will ride over the hill on a white charger and deliver inspiring proclamations wrapped in ribbon and a wax seal that will be read with town crier-enthusiasm to transform the organisation.

I remember sitting in the boardroom with the team, looking them in the eye and asking them to explore whether they felt that the excellence goal was a worthy challenge. They all agreed it was and that there was huge potential for improvement. Then I promised them that no one was coming. There was no help on the horizon. I suggested they had all the resource and talent to deal with this in the room where we sat. I asked what they were going to do to get things moving themselves. After a few moments' reflection, they realised it was up to them to take the initiative. They started with a simple definition of excellence and then each of them resolved to engage their teams in an immediate debate around process improvement. Significantly, they agreed a return date six weeks later to present progress on ideas they had implemented.

I was coaching a senior leader who was unhappy with her boss. It was annual review time, and my client was complaining that she was unable to cascade objectives to her own direct reports because she had not had any guidance or objectives from her line manager. This is a common complaint in organisations where employees believe they are unable to set clear objectives because of lack of clarity from above. So I suggested my client write a few objectives down, to second-guess the key issues for the organisation and to draft some herself, before sending them to her boss for review. Being accountable means taking the initiative and not waiting for the actions of others.

I was coaching a board member whose CEO had resigned, leaving a management team of three to look after the organisation. The business had a head office in Norway and the Norwegian owners were already on the case, searching for a successor. In the meantime, according to my client, a state of chaotic limbo had evolved. My client complained of the difficulty in managing through these uncertain times, how the management team felt directionless, and how the relationship with the Norwegian team appeared unstable and uncertain. We talked this through, and at first my client seemed to be taking a 'wait and hope' approach. He was worried that it could take up to six months to get a replacement CEO, and this interim period could be damaging to the business. I explored the actions he could take during this period that would at least help things to progress and I am delighted to report that he sorted it. And he sorted it with two well-crafted emails.

The first was to his colleagues. On the run up to a management meeting, he emailed them, asking for a special item to be added to the agenda. The agenda item was this:

Interim management: I think we need to face up to the fact that we are going to be without a leader over the next three to six months. This will create many challenges for us. What are we going to do to make sure we continue to run this business and build it while the search for a new CEO continues?

The second email was to the management team in Norway and it went like this:

I wanted to get in touch to discuss the interim leadership challenge resulting from the departure of our CEO. I know from experience it can take a while for new appointments to be made. So, I thought I would drop you a line to see what support you need from our management team, and how you would like to lead the business during this transition period.

Both emails were respectful but carried a clear call to action. What impressed everyone was that my client saw this as something he needed to help fix. The impact of this shift in mindset was profound. The leadership team began to work together to lead the business. They were open about the lack of clarity and how they had to lead through uncertain times. They were also open about their own feelings on the likely successor, and whether any of them wanted the job. Representatives from Norway were in touch with my client within an hour. They were delighted he took the initiative, invited him to a meeting and began to explore how they would best serve the interests of the company while searching for the CEO. And of course, this did my client's promotion prospects no harm at all.

Being accountable means living by the motto: **If not me, then who? If not now, then when?**

Yes, it is your problem; yes, you have the power to act; yes, you can pick this up; and yes, sometimes you have to confront tough realities. Oh, and yes, it is your crisp packet.

How to build a climate of accountability in your team

To build the appropriate mindset, you need to surround yourself with people who share your passion for accountability and your energy for getting things done. In no particular order, here are some ideas that will help to build a climate of accountability:

a) Spend time explaining the big picture to your team, more time than you think they need. They need to be crystal clear on their own goals, but they also have to be able to connect these to the departmental goals and the goals of the organisation. The clearer picture they have of the organisation, the better position they are in to help solve problems.

b) Ask a lot of questions. Become obsessed with the phrase 'What do you think?'.

c) Use team meetings to demonstrate an accountable mindset.

d) Make sure you banish any 'victim' or 'wait and hope'-style language from your own vocabulary.

e) Be prepared to confront the team with tough realities. Don't sugarcoat difficult times and difficult messages; they need to see the problems for what they are. So if costs are on the rise and there are hard times ahead, then you need to share these.

f) If people bring you problems to solve, send them away to think through some solutions first. Don't become known as the fount of all knowledge and the decision maker. Get people to think first and then discuss options.

g) Admit when you don't know the answer (and be prepared to admit this a lot). There are many variables in business coupled with a myriad of dependencies and outcomes. There are few 'right' answers, so don't pretend to be an expert.

h) Learn and apply some useful group problem-solving techniques. There are some really great ways to engage a team in collective problem solving. For example, check out the 'Work-Out' approach that was pioneered by Jack Welch in GE. A simple but effective way of group problem solving.

i) Discourage your team from using 'blame and complain' language. Pick people up on it when they use it.

j) Create some positive stories that demonstrate the favourable results you can achieve by being accountable.

k) Be proactive in working with other managers/leaders/ departments. Own the dependencies and take action to make things better.

l) When presenting on behalf of your team, there is a danger that you may be tempted to view things with rose-tinted spectacles. By all means celebrate your achievements and be confident in presenting how you are dealing with a problem, but don't be tempted to claim success for works in progress.

m) Break big problems into smaller chunks. For example, with a challenge as broad and expansive as 'building an excellence culture', give simple tasks, such as asking the team what they could do if they had five minutes to work on this today. Chances are they will start something sooner and spend longer on it.

n) Make sure your team meetings go into detail on progress

and problems. Ask for short presentations from each person on the progress they have made and what they need in terms of support from others.

o) When handing out projects, by all means be clear on who is leading each one. But do stress that you expect everyone to be supportive and involved.

p) Be wary of creating jobs that take away accountability. For example, creating a 'quality control manager' or a 'customer services manager' can encourage people to abdicate responsibility for important things. Words like 'quality' and 'service' need to be owned by everybody.

q) Beware giving people menial jobs. Tasks like coffee making, printing and collecting people from reception are often handed down to junior employees and in so doing, they expand and can occupy hours of time. Pitch in and help.

r) Keep the deadlines short. When your team is working on improvement points, set deadlines within the six to eight-week range. That is long enough to make progress on something, to take some initial steps and to observe some results. Be wary of projects that have deadlines set months away.

I like to use these three main headings to think through accountability:

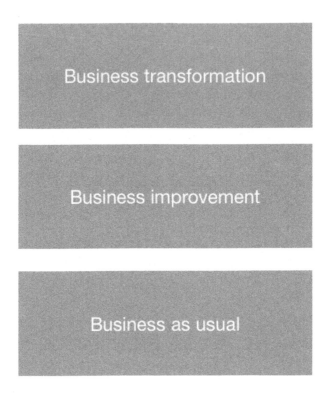

Fig 7 Levels Of Organisation Change

Business as usual

If people are working at this level, they come to work with a mindset of acceptance, tolerance and a view that things are okay as they are. Or, if they are not okay, someone else will probably sort it. People working at this level tend to keep their heads down and do the minimum. As a leader, you need to be out of this box yourself and do what you can to eliminate this mindset from your team.

Business improvement

Your team needs to be here. They need a mantra that says everything has unlimited potential to be better than it is, and they need to work constantly to make things better.

Business transformation

This is high-level thinking that challenges even the most fundamental assumptions you may have about how a business or market operates. You need to spend time here and encourage your team to join you.

Chapter summary

1. Building personal accountability is key in developing and building authentic credibility.
2. You need to role model the behaviour you would expect from others and challenge your team, direct reports and peers to seek solutions and focus on actions and results.
3. Sometimes you are faced with a tough reality that can't be changed. It is important to at least acknowledge this and identify the toolset you can work with.
4. Transformational change in organisations only happens if everyone feels responsible and accountable. Nothing happens while waiting for someone else to do something.

IMPACT

The first couple of minutes of any interaction matter. It is well documented that an interviewer will often make up their mind about a candidate almost instantaneously. If you think about it, you do the same. If your daughter brings home a new boyfriend, you quickly evaluate him against a mental list stored away somewhere of the ideal match. If you go shopping, your evaluation of the customer service is strongly influenced by first impressions and the opening few seconds of interaction.

So let's ask you a question and pause for a moment while you think about it.

What first and lasting impression do you create?

Let me be clear as we introduce this chapter: I am not adding more value to style over substance. We certainly don't want to encourage the growth of empty dullard leaders who happen to look the part. As we venture into an exploration of impact, we need the whole package. We want people who

- Look impressive
- Sound impressive
- Are impressive

It is not good enough just to work on the image and impact. With that in mind, let's dive into the more controversial and oft-debated part of the model.

Professional Image

I was running a workshop in a hotel and the CEO was due to arrive. I briefed the receptionist to expect her, and to direct her to our seminar room. The receptionist asked me how she would recognise her and I replied, 'Even if there are fifty people in the foyer, you could spot her.' Sure enough, when she arrived, the receptionist guessed our important guest's identity long before she introduced herself.

You can probably think of some people who create a similarly strong and positive first impression. How do they do that? Before I launch into advice and guidance on this one, I need to make a few high-level observations:

- o Different organisations have different approaches to dress code. What is seen as 'normal' in one organisation can be different in another.
- o An obvious and perhaps unfair or outdated point, but there is a difference between descriptors for professional image for men and for women.
- o I am aware of existing cultural differences that influence dress code and perceptions. I am writing this from the perspective of a European business mindset.
- o The choice is yours. When I coach people and this topic comes up, I don't insist that people change. Some organisations enforce dress codes, but there is always a huge range of choice about what to wear and how to present yourself. All I will do in this part of the book is to point out the things I believe build or indeed destroy executive presence. Whether you follow any of this advice is, of course, up to you.
- o Many organisations are taking steps to become less formal. Some have introduced 'dress down' days, while others actively discourage suits and ties in favour of more casual/informal attire.

Exploring Professional Image

Think about when you encounter someone for the first time. How quickly do you create a 'first impression' and what judgements do others make based on this? A series of experiments by Princeton psychologists, Janine Willis and Alexander Todorov, published in their article, First Impressions, in the July 2006 issue of Psychological Science, reveal that it takes a tenth of a second to form an impression of a stranger from their face alone. They also concluded that longer exposure to a face doesn't significantly alter that first impression.

We make fast judgments on:

- o   Whether we like them
- o   Whether we trust them
- o   Whether we could be friends
- o   Whether we find them attractive
- o   Whether we believe them to be aggressive

So, I am writing this on a train and from my seat I can clearly see two people. One is a professional female. She appears to be in her mid-thirties and is wearing large on-ear Sony headphones while watching a movie on her iPad. She has on a classy beige jacket with a simple black top underneath, and her hair is cut neatly. Her iPad is obviously one of the latest models, given the size of it. It has an expensive-looking cover portraying a map of the world. She is finding the programme funny and is trying to conceal a smile. I would say she is bright, well educated and she seems friendly and warm. I would like to work with her. In terms of career, I would put her in a leadership role and I imagine she works in a corporate role in a fairly substantial office.

Next to her is a guy I assume is in his fifties. He looks tired. He is wearing an open-neck blue shirt that is just visible underneath a dark blue V-neck jumper. Over that he wears a rather scruffy quilted jacket. He has a first generation iPad with a faded leather cover. He drifts in and out of sleep. He is slightly overweight. I would say that he is friendly, but perhaps tired of corporate life. I assume he is travelling on this train to get to work, but he has given up on the need to be early. I wouldn't choose him as a colleague, but he would be okay to share a beer with after work. In terms of status, I imagine him to be a technical professional, but not a person with a large team of people working for him. I imagine he is consulted on technical issues and presents summary documents of project progress. He is not in charge.

Of course, I have no idea whether I am right about either of the people sitting opposite me. But you try it. Next time you are in a public place surrounded by strangers, use your observational skills to review them and notice your response. People don't need to say anything, yet you leap to all sorts of conclusions about them.

The following pages explore some key topics that all contribute to personal impact:

   o   What you wear
   o   Visual destroyers of professional credibility
   o   A few thoughts on appropriate and professional dress code

This section is concerned with all things visible. We will explore what you say and what you think in later chapters.

Let's start with a few thoughts that apply regardless of the organisation. Do remember this book is about executive presence and building credibility at the most senior levels in an organisation.

Clothes matter

One of my company's clients is an IT consultancy, and we work closely with the senior team. It is a small organisation, but the management team share a few things in common. They are bright and professional. When you sit down with them, you feel instant respect for the whole team. However, when you leave the boardroom and walk through the main office, you wonder if the local pub has caught fire and, as part of the emergency evacuation procedure, all the people propping up the bar while watching the football over a pint have taken refuge in the office. The office is full of T-shirts, torn jeans and unwashed hair.

Now people will argue that the IT world is casual. They will mention Steve Jobs and his polo necks, the fact that Google has a value that says you don't need to wear a suit to do business. They will point to the need to be creative and how beanbags and pool tables create a relaxed atmosphere. It seems you don't 'dress down' in the IT world: the whole culture is based around comfort, casual clothing and an informal approach that people claim to be conducive to productive work. I get all that, but the place is shabby. There is a giant gulf between those on the top team and those working in the rest of the office. The people in the boardroom are not wearing business suits, but their shoes look clean, they are on the smart side of smart/casual and they look the part. If you were to wander through the office and I was to ask you to spot the members of the senior team, they would stand out a mile. Let me be clear: we are not making judgments about anyone's ability to do the work. But if you work in that organisation and want to progress, then maybe you need to dump the AC/DC T-shirt at some point.

Be smarter than your team

We are not talking about intelligence here, we are referring to dress code. As a general rule, a leader should stand out as more presentable than their direct reports. At least make the effort to set the standard.

I used to work with a head of communication who was very scruffy. His clothes were badly creased and his tie was stained. His credibility clearly suffered, as people discussed whether he was storing snacks on his clothing for mid-morning consumption. He did not set a good example for his department and, worse still, people could come to the conclusion that, if he couldn't dress properly, then he probably was poor at leadership.

Fit in with your environment and organisation

If you get on the train to Waterloo and head down to the Underground, you will spot dress code trends. Those working in and around Soho may well work in the creative industries, or specialist service firms. Here the dress code will often be less formal and more relaxed. Get on the Waterloo & City Line and head to the heart of the financial district, or travel to Canary Wharf, where many financial services firms have a significant presence, and the dress code changes. Here the code tightens up considerably. Business suits become the norm and cufflink shirts replace casual versions.

If you then get on a flight and head to Europe and venture into the financial sector in any given city centre, again the dress code will change. In some cases, it will be even more formal and in other cases, more relaxed.

I've learnt from my travels that there is no such thing as a universal dress code: you need to work out what is appropriate in your organisation and adapt accordingly. I was amused when running a senior VP programme in a Washington hotel by the sudden change in appearance from the participants on the programme. On Day One they were smart but casual, USA style.

Then on Day Two, everyone was 'suited and booted'. All the men were in smart suits and the women either in suits or otherwise smart outfits. I soon discovered that they had an early morning video conference with the CEO. Just thirty minutes. They had all dressed up for this. No one had briefed them, nothing was said the day before, but everyone understood the senior dress code when working at executive level. It is also worth bearing in mind that this was a five-day programme. Everyone had packed their suits and brought them across the USA for this single thirty-minute conference.

One of my clients has a straightforward dress code that seems to work pretty well: 'Dress for the day ahead'. In other words, make sure you are wearing the right outfit for the situation you face. This enables you to be more relaxed with just a day in the office and to dress more smartly when visiting customers.

Are clothes transformational?

I have no scientific evidence to support this next sentence and I am sure there are many exceptions, but let's put the statement out there.

There is a direct correlation between professional excellence and how people present themselves.

I work in consulting and maybe that is an unfair profession to discuss, but we recently ran a training programme helping people develop skills in executive coaching towards a qualification. The workshop was off-site in a hotel, so no one was with a client, and there was no formal dress code. A few people arrived wearing baggy jeans, sweatshirts and trainers, but a few had made a real effort to look smart. They perhaps still wore jeans but they fitted better; their shirts were of higher quality. Even accessories like notepads, pens, scarves and bags were more senior in look and feel. It was interesting to see how the style of coaching, the reading around the subject, the background knowledge, the preparation and even the performance in assignments were better for our smarter individuals. I don't believe the clothes made the difference per se, but what I noticed was that it was effort, preparation, thoughtfulness, respect and attention to detail that came through, not just in the clothes but in the attitude to the subject, the client and each other.

Most people divide a wardrobe into sections. There are clothes fit only for decorating the house, clothes for lounging around on a Saturday, clothes for a night out with friends, clothes to wear at a wedding and clothes to wear at work. In fairness, not everyone thinks like this. I know a couple of people who look the same regardless of their circumstances. If you were to bump into them as they left the house, you would be hard-pushed to tell what they were doing that day. In their mind, the Abercrombie & Fitch T-shirt and Levi's jacket meets every single clothing challenge.

There is something important about putting on a uniform and being ready for work. You should pay attention to what you are wearing, and I believe it does make a difference not only to your perceived credibility by colleagues but also to your sense of self-worth.

Does it cost a lot of money to dress well?

This is a good question. Let's consider the following matrix and what this can tell us:

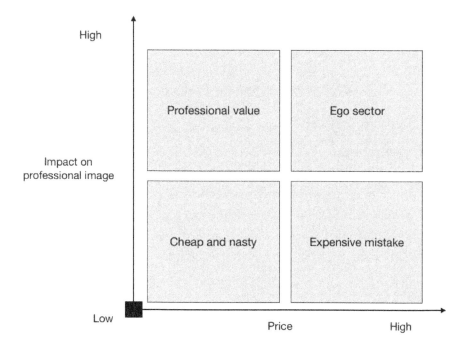

Fig 8 Price and Value Matrix

When buying clothes and accessories, you will always consider the variables of price and perceived value. This model is an adaption of a model by Dr Cliff Bowman at the Cranfield School of Management (hopefully he approves).

Cheap and nasty

You can buy cheap clothes that look great, but this box represents those that do not. Or the quality is awful. There is nothing wrong with saving money, but not at the expense of quality, look and feel.

Expensive mistakes

I recently spotted a man wearing a shirt that was mainly red in colour with large green maple leaf prints. He was standing in the reception area of a major financial services company. I suspect that his shirt was 'designer', but it looked ridiculous and out of place.

Professional value

You don't need to spend a fortune to look presentable. You need clothes that match, that fit and that feel right for the environment. You need to look like you have made an effort, and that doesn't mean spending hundreds or even thousands on clothes or shoes.

Ego sector

You can choose to pay a lot of money for whole outfits or accessories. Some are noticeable because of the famous brand, while others are not.

Destroyers of Professional Image

Smoking

If you are a smoker, you already know why this is on the list. Everyone knows it is a stupid habit. Even you. It is harmful for your health, antisocial, smelly and unpleasant. So how can we trust your judgement if you choose to do something that is so clearly bad for you? Even worse are the smokers who pretend they don't smoke or try to cover it up. They sneak outside for a cigarette, believing they can cover their tracks with a tic tac. They then waft into a meeting room, spreading the smell everywhere. They are quick to suggest a 'coffee break' so they can fuel their habit.

I believe all professional organisations should close all smoking areas and ban smoking in a mile-radius of the building. I visit plenty of companies and am often amazed that they allow the first impression of the business to be a bunch of smokers in a shed by the car park. I am not writing this book to make you give up smoking, but if you are a smoker:

1) GIVE UP SMOKING!
2) If you can't do that, then stop smoking during working hours.
3) If you can't do that, then please stop manipulating meetings to arrange smoke breaks. Everyone knows you are doing it.
4) Don't have a quick smoke on the way to a meeting. Use something else to repress the cravings, and avoid entering a room smelling like an old bonfire.
5) Collect a few used cigarette butts and put them in a cup of water. Give them a quick stir round and inhale deeply. That is what you smell like after a quick cigarette when you enter a room.
6) Smoke a cigarette in front of a mirror. Have a close look at yourself and see what you look like. It is unlikely that the image of James Dean or Cyd Charisse will appear.
7) Smokers often argue that during smoke breaks they network and connect with other people and that this is somehow a justification. How wrong they are. Nothing is more pathetic than a bunch of people huddling in the cold and the rain whilst taking a desperate drag on a cigarette.

Excessive drinking

This is an obvious one but worth exploring. Certainly in the City of London the drinking culture of old seems to have calmed somewhat. At one time, I can remember the underwriters popping down to a bar near Leadenhall Market for some three or four pints of Stella Artois at lunchtime. They would then return to work in a state that was hardly conducive to sharp thinking.

Perhaps one of the worst temptations for drinking is the away-day or the conference involving an overnight stay. Propping up the bar until the early hours and sharing an extensive bar tab can be seen as something of a rite of passage into the corporate inner sanctum.

Let's be clear, my company is a long way from tee-total. But we live by a few drinking 'rules' that serve us well. Firstly, we don't mix clients and alcohol. If we are working, we are working. We would not dream of having even a glass of wine before needing to be on duty. That includes any meeting or coaching session. Secondly, if you came along to one of our own off-site days where we were planning and collaborating internally, our refreshments at lunch would be sparkling water and juice. Our time together is precious and we don't blur our effectiveness by giving in to the temptation of a well-chilled Viognier.

In the evenings with clients, we will enjoy some wine. Sometimes more than would be safe to drive, but we do recognise that we are still at work. We are sociable, we engage in banter at the dinner table, but we do retire to bed feeling okay. And most definitely we are ready for anything the next morning.

My role takes me to many company off-sites. I recall with some amusement a guy called Stuart who drank so much at dinner that he took pleasure in removing all his clothes and running naked from tree to tree in the hotel grounds.

I remember the sales team who were up bright and early, ready to start Day Two of a workshop I was running when I had a realisation. They were not 'ready to start'; they were actually still in the bar at 7:00 a.m. The macho drinking culture had taken over and they had gone straight to breakfast. They were all being cool about this until about an hour later when one by one, they fell asleep through the morning sessions.

I remember Sarah, who drank to excess and spent the day groaning on a sofa in reception, too ill to contribute to the conference after a heavy night in the bar.

Tattoos and piercings

Tattoos and piercings have become much more mainstream and acceptable over recent years. Many footballers and musicians in the public eye are covered in tattoos. I have, however, put them in the 'destroyers of professional image' section for a reason. Some individuals are opposed to them and reject the idea of presenting customers with an image of a tattooed man or woman. Some are absolutely fine with them, but I need to raise a couple of 'red flags' just so that you are aware.

There are two historical perspectives that may help you to understand why tattoos got something of a bad name. In the UK, it was common for global explorers to adopt tattoos and piercings as they travelled the world. They would return to home shores with physical mementos of their travels. The dress code from the 1700s through to even the early 1900s was conservative. Men would wear full-length shirts and jackets, and women would wear dresses to cover their ankles. However, it was acceptable for the 'working man' to take off a shirt while working. Thus tattoos were often worn by many but only on show by the working classes and they began to be associated with working-class people.

The other perspective comes from criminal rebellion. In certain oriental cultures, crime was often punished by mutilation or amputation. A thief would have a hand removed as punishment for stealing, for example. As this barbaric treatment began to lose appeal in a civilised society, there were times when criminals were branded or tattooed as a deterrent to others. As a show of solidarity, other criminals would also adopt a tattoo and this created a message to non-tattooed people that tattoos are for those of a criminal disposition.

In today's society, there is no question that, for many, tattoos are seen as a sign of modern individualism and carry no stigma or negative connotations at all. But there are still some people in senior and influential positions who carry a deep-seated dislike of them. Now both sides would argue that they are right and in this book, I am to tread a neutral ground. My goal is for you to be aware that, if you are a fan of body art, you may well encounter someone who, rightly or wrongly, is not. Some organisations will not employ anyone in a front line or senior role who is visibly adorned with decorations and permanent piercings. You need to be aware of this and perhaps consider the advice that you have the ability to hide away any body art when you need to.

Know the dress code for your organisation

I have three anecdotes to demonstrate what I mean by this. Firstly, a newly appointed leader in a financial services office in the City arrived at work. His boss took one look at him and said something like, 'What on earth are you wearing?' He then reached forward, grabbed hold of the shirt pocket that was clearly visible beneath the suit jacket and tore it off the shirt. Apparently, shirt pockets were frowned upon and there was an expectation that shirts would be white, or business striped (mostly blue), with cufflinks instead of buttons and definitely no pocket on the front!

My second example is the senior leader who arrived for work in a brown suit, only to told by his boss, 'We don't wear brown in town so you had better go home and change.' The leader thought this was some kind of joke but one of his colleagues told him he had better follow the advice or he would not be allowed in the board meeting that afternoon.

The third example shows the opposite happening. A senior leader arrives suited and booted for his new role and discovers that suits and ties have been banned by the CEO, as the company is making a concerted effort to connect with a diverse and casually dressed workforce.

What we learn from these three examples are that dress codes can be extreme and your own assumptions about what is 'smart', 'acceptable' or 'normal' may be wrong.

Beware the 'dress down' invitation

I did some work for Lloyds Banking group and we had an off-site meeting for a full day and the dress code was 'business casual'. I arrived and luckily read this correctly. Everyone was dressed immaculately, but the gentlemen had removed their ties. That was the one concession to 'dressing down'.

Many organisations have 'dress down' days where employees are encouraged to wear more casual clothes, unless they have customer meetings to attend. Most people are aware they are still at work and err on the smart side of casual. There are some, however, who think this is a licence to delve into the very corners of the wardrobe and that the code brings legitimacy to the wearing of tat, awful colours, scruffy or ill-fitting outfits and in some cases, virtual pornography. I am often amused by the leadership team and what they wear in dress down days compared with the rest of the organisation. At one level we have smart trousers, smart shirts/blouses and jackets. And at the other, we have beachwear and stupid T-shirts bearing slogans that weren't funny when they were first purchased.

Weight issues

This is a sensitive point but needs saying. I know some people have weight problems due to medical conditions. I am also aware that many are carrying the weight of too many lunches, snacks and dinners around their midriff. Being seriously overweight can send a signal that suggests lack of self-care, lack of control and lack of concern. And that is wholly undesirable when trying to establish executive presence.

There are many definitions of being 'overweight', but for a quick and simple view, weigh yourself (especially if you haven't done so for a while) and then type 'BMI' into Google. There are plenty of free ways to calculate your Body Mass Index. The NHS service is helpful here. When you enter your height, weight, age and gender into the form, the website will provide an instant statement of your current body mass and a target weight for your height. If your BMI is too high, consider revising your diet and exercise regime to see how you can present a healthier appearance.

Cleavage and underwear

One of my more awkward moments came when coaching a female for promotion to a senior role. She was bright, for the most part professional, with a great track record ... but she was wearing an outfit that left very little to the imagination. The cut of her blouse would have been inappropriate in most business environments. As a bloke coaching a professional female, it presented a challenge, as I felt I needed to say something, despite the embarrassment it would cause. Anyway, I decided to wait until the next time I saw her. At that point, I told her, 'I need to mention something that was bothering me when we met last time.' 'It was the outfit, wasn't it?' she replied. It turned out she had realised the top was too revealing, and all it took from me was a prompt for her to admit it.

I am no expert in female dress code but I do think I am qualified to mention the low-cut outfit as a destroyer of professional credibility. Along with one other key gripe of mine, which is women who show their underwear at work. There are various ways to do this and I have no doubt you have seen them all too.

The 'English Blouse' is well known in Europe. It is the European description of a translucent white blouse that is so see-through that the bra can be easily seen underneath. Especially if the colour is darker or brighter. Then there is the blouse that is either too tight or has a cut that means the underwear is visible every time the wearer moves.

A simple rule of thumb: if other people can see your underwear, it is not professional, so cover it up.

Tips for professional wear at work

Keep things clean

It goes without saying that clothes need to look clean and tidy. Suits need to be pressed, shirts clean and fresh. Few things destroy credibility more than evidence of dried food on clothing. Men are often the worst offenders here, with shoes that are in desperate need of a polish. It does mean packing extra clothing for business trips to guard against heading off to work in a shirt stained with coffee from a spillage at the breakfast table.

How do you smell?

At one end of the spectrum we have the stench of body odour (clearly not pleasant for anyone in the office). At the other end we have overpowering aftershaves and perfumes. No one appreciates working with smelly colleagues. The great unwashed come to work and think they can get away with few showers and no deodorant. They can't!

Accessories matter

When you think about image, everything counts. People notice the obvious like clothing and shoes and the things you might not pay much attention to, such as bags, pens, notebooks.

If you sit down in the boardroom, it's not a good look to pull a tired and well-thumbed notebook from a rucksack and scribble with a chewed Bic biro. I had a coaching client who arrived with a notebook clearly designed for children's drawings, so I brought it to her attention. She was quite defensive about her notebook, but the next time I saw her she was carrying a nice 'leather' folio, which I commented on. It turns out that it cost her £2.97 from a local supermarket (proving that perceived quality isn't necessarily expensive). She was also embarrassed to admit that three people had complimented her on the new notebook, which proved that people had noticed the change.

As a simple test for yourself, have a look at everything you take to work. Include any accessories you carry with you and might take out at a meeting. Mentally score it according to your perception of the professional fit with a boardroom. For example, you may like your waterproof rucksack and find it convenient and fit for purpose. Could you imagine the CEO arriving with it? My advice is that everything you carry with you should be representative of the brand and image you are trying to present to the world. I believe you should be consistent and raise the bar on your own standards. As my coaching client discovered, perceived class didn't require a trip to the Smythson shop for her stationery, but it did require thought and effort.

Be smart and presentable no matter what the dress code says

My advice is to be wary of words like 'dress down' and casual. By all means relax what you wear, but these words do not signal that it's acceptable to put the old gardening trousers on. For men that means nice, well-polished shoes. A stylish shirt with long sleeves is best and cufflinks are better. Smart dark trousers or good quality and well-fitted jeans. Make sure you visit the barber every six weeks or so. A good jacket always finishes off the look.

Suits are still the norm in many organisations and if that is true of your organisation, make sure you are measured once in a while and get a good fit. They need regular dry cleaning. In many places, many men now remove their ties and wear an open shirt. That's fine, of course, but if you are in tie-wearing land, make sure it is a nice one. In general, wide ties look old fashioned. Silk always carries class and if the suit is not the most expensive, perhaps a quality tie will lift the whole outfit. Whatever you do, don't think it is a good idea to wear cartoon ties. I remember a manager with a picture of Bart Simpson on his. Nothing says 'sad pathetic person with no sense of humour' more accurately than wearing a tie featuring a cartoon character. If your shirt carries a lot of pattern, be wary of a tie with too much pattern and vice versa. In general they should work well together.

I mentioned the phrase 'don't wear brown in town' earlier and there is a belief that brown suits don't carry as much class. I tend to agree (and I know others disagree). I do believe that a dark suit with a white shirt and impressive silk tie carries a lot of class. In fact, this combination is pretty tough to beat.

For women, the dress code is far more complex because there are so many variations in clothing options and expectations. The last decade has also seen a relaxation of some of the more formal expectations with dress code, which has resulted in a myriad of options. At one time, a business woman would be expected to have a wardrobe full of perfectly tailored suits with well-fitting blouses to match. Today expectations can be far more casual. In general terms, the unwritten rules for women are similar to those for men. Despite all the changes in dress code and fashion, it is interesting to see how professional many women appear in the senior corridors of power.

There are a few pointers that are worth thinking through. Do with these what you will:

- Good quality, classic items are worth investing in.
- Make sure clothes fit well, especially around the shoulders, and that blouses do not gape or are too tight over the bust area.
- Darker, plain suits still work best when it comes to smart dressing. That's not to say you must avoid all colours and flashes of style, but be wary of overly outlandish colours and patterns.
- Blazers or jackets look much smarter than cardigans. I know cardigans can help keep you warm on a chilly day, but most look over casual.
- Scarves can add a classy flare to an outfit. It is worth investing in a couple of elegant scarves, as these tend to be highly visible.
- Colour coordination between shoes, bags and belts adds a professional touch.
- Beware ridiculously high heels. By all means wear something comfortable on your feet to get to work, but don't keep the trainers on all day.
- It is best not to wear open-toed shoes to work. Keep the open toes for the beach. If you must wear them, make sure toenails are well groomed.

Beards

Another controversial subject, this section includes facial hair for men. At the time of writing, there seems to be a wide adoption of full facial beards and moustaches amongst professional men. Obviously, that is a personal choice, but do be aware that the full beard covers up many facial expressions. So you need to smile more with a beard or moustache than you might without one. If beards are your thing, keep it trimmed and neat. Don't allow it to become to uncontrolled.

Walking tall

A key part of first impressions is based on how you enter a room. Many people are guilty of entering a room and demonstrating, perhaps unintentionally, that they would rather be somewhere else. Here are some top tips for entering a room with style:

- Do be on time, if not respectfully early. You should never be late for important meetings, so don't make a habit of this. Being late means you are more likely to be unfocused, ill prepared and to look chaotic.

- Don't use your phone just before the meeting. No matter how bored you are waiting, don't be tempted to check your emails or social media. You may read something that may distract, upset or annoy you, which could knock you off your stride. But there is more to it than that. When you are using your phone, your arms will be tucked in, your head will be down. This physiology mirrors the body posture we might adopt to show lack of confidence or disappointment. The message this sends is not lost on your brain, so don't do it.

- Don't fill your head with negative thoughts before the meeting. If, deep down, you are worried about something, don't let this thought spin around your head before you walk in (more on this in the 'Ego State' chapter).

- Do use the legend-building technique on yourself. Think of the most positive outcome and bring the questions 'What do you want people to think feel, say, do?' to life in your head.

- Do control your breathing. Take a moment before you come into the room to calm yourself. A couple of deep and slow breaths can help.

- Do adjust your posture so that you sit up straight and walk tall.

- Do greet people positively. Stand up, walk around and offer a handshake.

- Don't offer a 'killer grip' handshake or a 'damp lettuce leaf' (more on this later).

- Do make an effort to introduce yourself to people you know less well.

- Don't hide behind people you feel comfortable with. There is a tendency for people to gravitate towards the familiar faces in the crowd.

- Do be attentive and courteous to others. This means being kind and considerate even with the simple things. Pour the water, offer your seat, open the doors.

- Don't sit there on your laptop or your phone. This sends a terrible signal to everyone else in the room that you don't care about them.

- Don't gabble and talk too fast.

- Do beware the buffet with impossible-to-eat food. Keep things simple.

Chapter Summary

Let's conclude this section on visual impact with a few thoughts and questions for your consideration:

1. What you wear matters more than you think. What are you communicating with your clothes?

2. Organisations can be very different in terms of dress code, norms and rules. How does what you wear compare with the most senior and impressive people in the organisation? If you want a seat at the table, you need to look the part.

3. Your personal brand is visible and you carry it to every meeting. Imagine you are going to a meeting. Put everything you would carry, show or use on the table in front of you: notebooks, pads, pens, pencils, bags, scarves. Add your business card to the pile as well. Now review it from an executive perspective. What does it say about you and your brand?

4. There is a big difference between being impressive and trying too hard to impress people. Be authentic, confident and credible.

5. Body language matters a great deal. What does your body language and behaviour say about your levels of confidence? What visual cues do other people pick up from you?

Social Skills

Let's start this section by using a quote from Stephen Covey concerning social skills and executive presence:

'Most people don't listen with the intent to understand. They listen with the intent to reply.'

This statement says a lot about the mindset for executive presence. There is something quietly impressive about people who ask more, who listen more, who seek to connect rather than pronounce their knowledge and unload it onto people. Impressive people are excellent connectors, and thrive in a room full of people. Many readers will have delved into preference theory and will have strong self-awareness about their communication style. There is a common misconception that extroverts have an advantage when it comes to social skills. That is simply not the case. Social skills are part mindset, and part skills and behavioural based.

I have never met him, but I have been impressed by every description I have heard and read about Bill Clinton. I know that famous people have the edge when it comes to making an impression on a room, but Bill is famous not only for being 'Mr President' but also for his skill and craft in connecting with people. He lives by a phrase that comes from Africa: Sawubona. Translated, this means 'I see you'. Living by Sawubona principles means spotting and recognising everyone in the room and acknowledging them. Not just the important ones and the ones right in front of you, but the ones in the background. This includes receptionists, cloakroom assistants, cleaners, in fact anyone who becomes a blip on the periphery of your personal radar.

The response to Sawubona is 'Ngikhona', which means 'I am present' – an acceptance that the greeting has been received and the whole person is now here. A significant part of social skills is based around the idea that you are more interested in other people and what they have to say than being boastful about yourself.

As an introduction to my executive programme, I discuss the incredible power and influence of coaching skills on life. These skills are the greatest building blocks of excellence in leadership, and I would encourage all readers to grasp every opportunity to build and develop their own craft as a coach. One of the gurus in the coaching world is Sir John Whitmore, who wrote Coaching for Performance. He published a tweet in 2014 that said, 'A coaching style should be the norm for conversations.' This strong statement is worthy of consideration.

When we adopt a coaching style:

- We are more interested than attempting to be interesting.
- We listen more than we talk.
- We have respect for other people's stories rather than a desire to tell our own.
- We are fascinated by in-depth conversations rather than keeping things superficial.
- We love to ask 'what do you think' rather than explain our own thoughts.
- We believe people learn a lot about you while you learn a lot about them.

Be In The Room

The starting point for improving social skills is not to shy away from people. You need to enter a room and be mindful of those present. My business often attends trade shows and we put up a stand to attract new business opportunities. Delegates from the conference wander along corridors of exhibition stands and then disappear into the spaces reserved for those paying to be there. As someone at one of these events with a sales mindset, when I spot someone approaching, I confess to an inner dialogue that often talks me out of starting a conversation. I tell myself that the person approaching is probably too busy or not interested, or seems to have the wrong profile for the sort of person who might need our services. Often this dialogue will let people pass me by. Well, that was until I went to a seminar that presented a startling fact. In a survey of conference delegates, the majority complained that too few people had been bothered about talking to them. It turns out that, whilst the body language or style seemed to suggest lack of interest, that was their way of dealing with a lack of confidence in social skills. All they needed from me was a quick hello and a 'what brought you to the trade show today?' And most people were delighted to stop for a chat.

How true that is for every conference or meeting you may have attended. People disguise their own lack of social skills by appearing busy, looking through their phones or scanning papers. You can break the ice by simply walking up to them and saying 'Hi, I don't think we have met. I'm Andy, tell me what brings you here.' The mindset you need to be impressive is a genuine curiosity to connect with other people in the room. Especially those who are new to you. Of course, once you start a conversation, you also need to express genuine interest in them.

Genuine interest in others

On my company's training programmes, we run a simple but effective test. We ask people to bring to mind a problem that is bothering them or something they need to think through. We then ask them to take some time on their own and to note down how long they can focus on something before their mind wanders. If you have a few moments to spare, why not have a go yourself. Just pick a topic and get a watch out and open the timer. Start the clock and then begin to process your problem and, as soon as your mind wanders off topic, make a note of how long you lasted. When we do this on training programmes, few participants last longer than sixty seconds before their mind wanders off topic. Thoughts and distractions get in the way, and stop us from thinking things through.

A coaching conversation style means that you 'hold the space' for someone. It means asking a question and remaining interested and inquisitive in a way that keep people focussed and on topic. Significantly, the time you spend together is not about you. You can't fake this, and you need to live by the following motto that I picked up from an advanced coaching seminar by Aboodi Shabi:

'Abandon your expertise and welcome your curiosity.'

What a lovely sentiment that is. Think about the implications this motto carries for many of the social interactions you experience. Deep down, you know it makes sense. We have all been 'sold to' by a salesperson who insists on telling you about the features and benefits of their product without first understanding our buying needs. We have all spent time with a manager who is keen to explain how to fix a problem before they spend any time understanding the real issue. We have all been to meetings where all we need is a pen and blank sheet of paper to make a note of things, as no one ever asks for our opinion.

In its simplest form, when we are working a room full of strangers, this motto gives us permission to discover more about people and to share less about ourselves. Of course, you can share information if people ask, but don't take a simple question from a colleague as licence to wax lyrical about yourself.

Bette Midler's quote from the film Beaches comes to mind here. Bette is a legendary extrovert and exuberant over-the-top personality. In the movie, her character, CC, speaks at length about herself, pauses for breath and says, 'Anyway, that's enough about me, let's talk about you. What do you think of me?' This statement carries a lot of humour in the context of the movie, but it's something for you to be mindful of when establishing executive presence.

If you want to build credibility and gravitas, be more interested in others and less interested in telling them about yourself.

Listen and listen harder

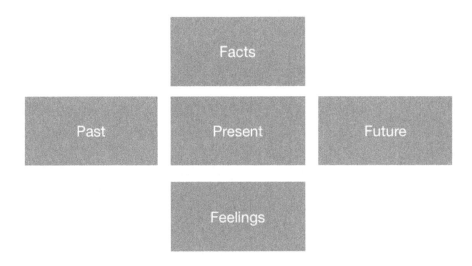

Fig 9 Interviewing - Getting the Whole Picture

This diagram represents a simplistic view of a personal problem. We have a timeline of past, present and future, and then two surrounding considerations: the facts and the feelings. Therefore, in a conversation when someone describes a problem, you have the potential to ask the following questions:

- What issue are you working on?

- Tell me about the origin of the project. How did this start?
- What's happening now?
- What have you done?
- What options are you thinking about?
- How did you feel when you started?
- How do you feel now?
- What is resting on this? How important is this to other people?
- What do you think you will do going forward?
- How confident do you feel?

In other words, this simple model maps a respectful territory. Sadly, most leaders fail to grasp this respect, and instead they do this:

Fig 10 The Leap to Advice

What happens in most cases is that the merest mention of a problem is met with a solution along the lines of, 'Here is what you should do based on my experience of dealing with things.' In other words, the leader sees themselves as the expert, the sage, the fount of all knowledge and the one with all the answers. Their goal is to get this problem off the table as fast as possible, and to move on to something else.

Developing great social skills is about respect for other people's stories and a genuine desire to learn more and understand more. You are more impressive as a thinking partner than an advisor. People love to talk things through, and few problems are solvable with a simple pearl of wisdom from you.

The key to listening is all about having a genuine desire to hear more and understand what is going on. You want the whole picture and you need to get a sense of the emotions and the facts, and how these are mixed up.

Try it. Next time you go to a meeting or a one-to-one, liberate yourself from the role of expert. You absolutely do not need to solve any problem people bring you. All you need to do is to understand the whole thing in more depth, including how everyone feels about it. Then see where that takes you. I believe you will be seen as more impressive as a result and you will learn a lot more about your colleagues.

There is one other key part of listening that is worth mentioning here.

Summarising is a powerful leadership tool

Yes, summarising rather than concluding or advising. When Meredith Belbin did his research into team roles back in the 1970s for his 1981 publication, Management Teams: Why They Succeed or Fail, he looked at the whole arena of what he called 'natural leadership'. He began to explore the behaviours and characteristics of the people who seemed to influence the direction of their group. Belbin fine-tuned this research over time and developed the core of his team role theory. If you read through the current research, you will find one of the key roles in helping a team to make progress is that of 'chairman', and the symbol used for this character is a conductor holding a baton. It is significant that the orchestra conductor doesn't play an instrument. But key to successful chair skills are summarising and clarifying. Belbin recognised the power of the person who summarised progress, who checked in with people, who helped people focus on the areas they agreed on. For anyone wanting to establish executive presence in a leadership role, the implication is clear. See at least one of your main tasks as a summariser. Listen to stories, experiences; listen for the emotions that go with them. You become a powerful leader when you use words like, 'I can see this has been a struggle for you' as opposed to, 'Well, if I were you...'

Social Graces

I also need to point out a few social graces and considerations that go a long way to building credibility and presence. I am sure you are aware of most of them, but consider this a memory jog:

Greeting people: Always start with a smile. We often underestimate the power this has in putting people at ease. Have a look at the faces of people attending a meeting when someone is presenting. A management representative can often present a grumpy and stern persona that doesn't inspire confidence.

Names: People love it when you remember their names. Some people argue that they are not good at this, but it simply needs practice. Use a notebook and draw mini table plans for yourself. When my company runs training programmes that last over several months, we often take a photo and make notes in the margin to act as a memory jogger for names in the group. When running a workshop for even fifty people, we aim to lock all the names into our recall memory by coffee break. It can be done!

The little things: Guests who stay in the very best hotels often express surprise when the employees appear to remember the finer details from a previous stay. Preferences for drinks, newspapers and rooms are often recalled with a flourish as part of the experience of five-star luxury. Of course, the hotel staff don't really spend all day memorising faces and preferences, they have a simple IT system that logs these details for whenever a guest checks in. Still, there is something in this attention to detail that is impressive. Think about it for a moment and recall the small details you are aware of about the people close to you. If you have a PA or a leadership team, what can you remember about birthdays, special events, children, house moving, sport allegiance, etc, of those close to you? If you want to be impressive, don't just remember someone's name. Ask specific questions that show you remember them as a person. Oh, and not for effect, but because you mean it.

Handshake: My dad used to obsess about this and advise on a 'firm grip, straight up and at right angles to the body, offered with confidence and good intentions'. Sound advice. As a reminder, we shake hands to demonstrate trust and a willingness to connect at the most basic of levels. In the days of early man, open palm gestures were used to show that we were not carrying any weapons. The handshake developed as a positive statement of equality and the meeting of equals. So make sure you develop a good handshake. Why not get some feedback on yours? We don't want the weak, limp lettuce leaf-style of shake that feels horrible and pathetic, nor should the crush of your hand leave the recipient wondering if they need to pop to the Accident & Emergency ward for an X-ray for fear of broken bones. With handshakes, do make the effort to connect with people and take the lead. Women are often reluctant to get involved in this ritual, and can be guilty of remaining in a seat while men go through the standing up and shaking hands part of the meeting. Consider it part of the core greeting and get involved.

Just one other word of warning on handshakes. Don't offer a dominant hand to someone. This is where you turn your 'shaking' hand over slightly (palm down), which forces your colleague to twist their own palm up. This is a domineering gesture and you should avoid it at all costs.

Noticing and consideration: Pay attention to the people in the room. Offer teas and coffees and show kindness. If someone has driven a long way, make sure they have a chance to grab a drink before a meeting. I am coaching someone at the moment and to get to the session, I am in the car for over an hour. We meet in a room by the café in the main building and not once have I been offered a drink. And yes, I have mentioned it to my client. He seemed surprised, but I explained that I extrapolated his behaviour. If he didn't offer me a coffee after a long drive for an important occasion, I wondered how kind and considerate he was to his staff on a day-to-day basis.

Meeting space: When you sit at a meeting table, make sure you land well and take up enough space, but don't overwhelm the table. This may be an unfair generalisation, but men often spread papers and accessories widely, while women find themselves fighting for space.

Meeting etiquette: I remember running a workshop in France for a senior leadership team. I arrived first and gradually all the participants arrived and took their places around the U-shaped conference table. Before they sat down, they each plugged in a laptop, creating a spaghetti of cabling on the floor in the middle of the room. They all wanted the Wi-Fi code and began to type – continually. The CEO in particular was a great one for typing while the meeting was in progress. I asked about this and was assured that this multi-tasking was normal. As the person trying to facilitate the session, it was what I would describe as a tough gig. I was never sure who was engaged and who was disengaged. It soon became apparent that they were pinging emails to each other as well as the outside world. I found it hard to work with them, difficult to raise interesting questions and almost impossible to meet the terms of the brief they contracted me in for. Now perhaps this was an exception, but you have no doubt been to meetings where people constantly type on phones, laptops or tablets.

The behaviour isn't constructive or appealing.

I am wise enough to appreciate that technology has changed. Many people have traded the pad of paper for an iPad. It is common for meetings to put a sign up with a social media hashtag to encourage debate and discussion beyond the conference room. In other words, there are some circumstances when typing away is acceptable. But you need to manage this. I think you can tell the difference between someone who is typing a few meeting notes on an iPad and someone who is responding to emails. One manager of a senior leadership programme seemed completely pre-occupied with WhatsApp the whole time he was in the room. It was so obvious that the other delegates mentioned it to me. I discussed it with him. He made an attempt to justify his behaviour and just carried on doing it. He argued, 'We do this all the time where I come from'. What I observed was a leader who seemed disconnected on every level. His behaviour meant that he didn't engage in debate, he seemed oblivious to the contribution and questions of others, and it seemed that he would rather be somewhere else.

So my advice for you is to set the example for meeting etiquette. Minimise your own use of technology and encourage your colleagues to do the same. This is especially true if you invite someone into a meeting from outside. Management teams can appear so disrespectful to people when a presenter is met by a sea of faces all typing to people who are not in the room.

The business lunch: If you are booking a lunch, here are a few of the polite rules that you should bear in mind when hosting a gathering.

- The ideal time for lunch is 13:00.
- Make sure you get there earlier than your guests.
- You need to take charge of the timing and the seating, and should be proactive in moving people to the table.
- Help to guide your guests through the menu. Ask them whether

they would like starters or just mains, and follow their lead.

- Whatever you do, don't allow a guest to be the only one ordering a starter or desert. Always join them if they take the initiative.
- Take charge of the wine list yourself, including ordering wine.
- House wine is fine in most nice restaurants. Only order more expensive wine if you really know the list well and are looking for something in particular.
- Never order expensive wine unless you are paying for it.
- Don't ask to taste house wine when offered.
- Don't be the only person who opts for alcohol with lunch. Again, take the lead from your guests.
- Tap water is fine in the UK.
- Never double dip food! You may find this acceptable at your family dinner table but it is not okay in formal company.
- Don't pause between mouthfuls and hold both sets of cutlery in one hand.
- Line up your cutlery neatly on the plate to signal you have finished eating.
- Beware of booking lunch in a pub or more informal restaurant where the norm is to order food and drinks from the bar. If you are hosting the event, you may find yourself stuck at the bar for far too long, leaving your guests waiting at the table.
- Don't ask your guests if they are enjoying the meal. You should have chosen a restaurant where the quality and presentation of the food is of a high standard, and you would expect them to be saying how nice everything is.
- Make sure you manage the bill. Take charge of asking for it and settling it. Never get into a debate on who had what to eat and how much people should pay if you are splitting it.
- Tipping the waiter is always a good idea. In some countries it is expected (the USA is the obvious land of excessive tipping). But good service deserves a tip, usually ten to twenty per cent.

Body language and social skills

Finally, a few words on body language. In our section on impact, I talked about the need to walk tall into a room and to land well. There are a few body language errors that are worth pointing out. I have to confess these are generally male body language issues.

Sitting with folded arms: I know many will claim this gesture is comfortable, but it can send a signal of being disinterested.

Arms clasped behind your head: This is often perceived as a dominating gesture that people use to demonstrate the upper hand. I recall with some amusement attending a seminar run by body language guru, Allan Pease. He condemned this gesture and suggested that, if anyone does it to you, you should copy it and see who gives up soonest. I am not sure you should run a dominant body language competition but the gesture isn't polite in a business setting so, if you catch yourself doing it, try to change the posture.

Sitting with legs wide open (the crutch display!): This one is definitely a male gesture and is done by sitting on a chair with your legs wide open and facing someone. Just don't do this.

Eating while getting down to business: I know that a lot of business meetings involve lunch, buffets, biscuits and cakes,, and I am certainly not about to banish light refreshments from your calendar. I run programmes aimed at developing people as executive coaches, and the advice on the programme is not to eat while coaching. In fact, the only refreshment I order with my coaching hat on is a glass of water. I think it is hard to listen properly and difficult to show authentic attention whilst balancing a plate of buffet food. Where you can, take breaks for lunch and keep the time for eating and chatting as informal. If you do have to combine the two, keep it light and simple.

Chapter Summary

1. Social skills and emotional intelligence are key in developing relationships with others.
2. Building trust and openness is essential, and to do this you need to demonstrate an open style and to listen more than you talk.
3. Don't leap too quickly to offer your advice. Helping people to think things through is much more effective over time.
4. Develop your coaching skills, as these will be transformational to your one-to-one sessions and to your meetings.
5. There is tremendous power in summarising people's thinking and where differences of opinion reside.
6. Make sure you are aware of the rules of etiquette when out for lunch.

Inspirational Presenter

Let's return to the core question here. Would you rather go to the board meeting with a mediocre idea and a compelling presentation, or an amazing idea and a poor presentation and style? Where are you on this diagram?

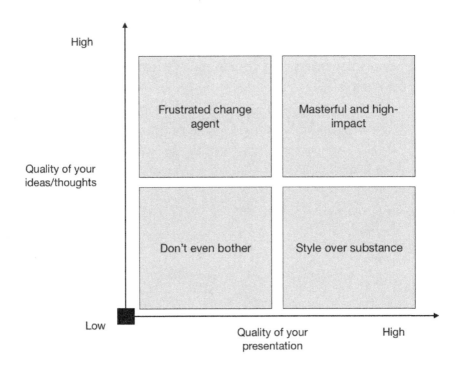

Fig 11 Proposal and Presentation Matrix

I recall working with a bright guy, whom we will call Gordon. He had an impressive grasp of financial data, and his thinking was clear and eloquent. But put him in a room with a data projector and a laptop for ten minutes, and he could drive even a rational human being to question their need to live. He was dull, uninspiring and was, as a consequence, continually frustrated by his lack of progress and buy-in from the most senior levels in the business. He would complain about the executive team, but in reality, the problem was his own lack of style in putting his ideas across.

Another client of mine was being considered for a significant promotion, but his CEO had given him some hard-hitting feedback about his need to be strategic and to rise above the detail. I met my client a couple of times and found him to be pretty impressive. Then I asked him to show me a draft presentation he was preparing for a big meeting with the board. As soon as I saw his preparation, I could see the problem. He had prepared pages and pages of detail. Slides were numerous, busy and complex, and he used too many words and a poor structure. When I quizzed him about the slide deck, he became defensive. I learnt that he'd once presented to a senior group, and had been asked a couple of probing questions around the detail. This fazed him, so he resolved to solve the problem by putting every ounce of detail into future presentations. He left nothing out. Every chart, number, idea and thought was included. As a result of this revised presentation style, his boss gave him the feedback that he lacked the capacity to rise above a problem and take a strategic view.

Now, as usual in this book, we might consider that an unfair statement. But that is what we are dealing with: people are unfair, and they make judgements based on their experience.

So let's explore the four quadrants of the model for a moment.

1) **Don't even bother**: This is a harsh statement, but my advice is that you don't stand up to present if you have nothing to say and are lousy at presenting. Sadly, this doesn't stop people, as I have no doubt many readers will have suffered at the hands of such presenters. The trouble is that the quality of your presentations matters a great deal. Deliver a well-structured and carefully thought-through presentation and people will believe you are an impressive leader. The opposite is also true. If you feel you are truly in this box, then either get someone else to do the presentation or cancel it.

2) Style over substance: Some people have the gift of the gab and can present anything with style and enthusiasm. I have seen terrific slides, passion, strategies, ideas and proposals all revealed with the touch of a magician. I can recall an exceptional strategic business planning presentation that was a joy to behold. It was designed, developed and delivered by a slick management team who quickly established themselves as formidable. A couple of weeks later, the director was fired along with his director of finance. It transpired that there were huge holes in the accounts, and no amount of bravado could disguise the fact that the team were, in fact, 'flogging a dead horse', as the CEO so eloquently put it. The same CEO announced a longing for authenticity instead of well-managed and engineered BS.

3) Frustrated Change Agent: I mentioned Gordon in the introduction to this section, and he falls into this category. Promising ideas but poorly packaged and presented. People do pay attention to the packaging and presentation, and Gordon needs to learn that the presentation of ideas is as important as the ideas themselves.

4) Masterful and High Impact: Obviously this is the place to be. Great ideas are presented well, and the whole package has strong, authentic and compelling credibility.

So how do you ensure you exist most of the time in Box 4? Here are some tips that I believe will make a difference:

Preparing yourself in advance

Skill building: Enrol on a high-quality presentation skills programme. Choose wisely and make sure you are working with credible facilitators. Look for a good track record of working with senior people.

Feedback: Whenever you do a presentation, request feedback. But make sure you come at this from two important perspectives. Firstly, spend time understanding what people liked about your style, content and approach. Secondly, explore the 'even better if...' areas. Every single presentation has the potential to be better than it is, so search for your development needs. Be wary of just getting positive feedback and believing you have arrived as one of the world's best presenters. Most people lie to you when you ask them how your presentation went. You see someone leave a conference platform and over coffee, people will tell them how much they enjoyed their session. This is (possibly) true, but many people are polite and tell you what you want to hear. Seek out anonymous feedback and ask those you trust to critique your work.

Don't busk important moments: If you have anything important to present, then put some decent preparation time into it. For example, if you are to be on your feet for thirty minutes at a conference, get your team together for a half day a couple of times to pull the themes and ideas together and rehearse it. Oh, and rehearsal means rehearsal. You need to speak the words, show the slides and experience the timing. Don't be tempted to think that reading slides on a laptop is enough. You need to walk the presentation through in real time to develop and improve it.

Design matters

Take an artistic and creative view of your slides and your material. Test each slide or piece of written material by using these (or similar) questions:

- **Readable**: Can people actually read the writing and the words? The font size needs to be big enough to be read in a large room.
- **Clear**: Does every slide contain a clear key point?
- **Interesting**: Does the design and format look interesting and appealing?

- **Less is more**: Challenge the number of words on your visuals. If you have whole sentences or even paragraphs of text, you definitely have scope to reduce these. Seth Godin (guru and most impressive speaker) advocates no more than six words per slide. That is hard to achieve all the time, but it's a worthwhile challenge.
- **Does it flow and feel professional?** With this in mind, beware the dreaded animations, builds and presentation effects that come with the software. For example, I can press a button on my laptop and my slide will burst into little stars and reform as if by magic into new words. This is only vaguely interesting the first time, and after a couple of presses, it looks cheap and annoying. Personally, I don't use animations at all.
- Find pictures that sum up what you want to say.
- If you have to present figures and numbers, then make the important ones really stand out. Don't hide them away or clutter them with irrelevance.

Preparing yourself on the day

- What do you want your audience to think, feel, say or do at the end of your presentation? Think this through before you start.
- Be an hour early and don't allow the panic of 'just made it in time' show on your face.
- Create a positive mental picture before you start – imagine a fully engaged and attentive audience.

Own the room

You can't always choose where to present, but do remember these points:

- Heating, lighting and air-conditioning are all important. Do what you can to make the room feel comfortable.
- I take a room spray with me to fragrance the room before people arrive. I never mention this to people, but I want

their senses to be aware that the room feels fresh and inviting. Jo Malone's Lime, Basil & Mandarin is a favourite, in case you were wondering.

- Keep things nice and tidy. Don't leave random bags, used coffee cups and general stuff on show.
- You want to connect with people, so don't stand behind the podium if there is one. Lecterns are for preachers in churches and sermons.
- Pay attention to where you stand and where you sit. Above all, reduce the space or barriers between you and the audience.
- Think about when to hand things out if you have them, and make sure they are within easy reach.

Your introduction

Your first minute is critical, so make sure you start well. Any audience will be attentive when a new person starts speaking.

- Stand tall.
- Bring energy and enthusiasm to the start. Take a breath, steady yourself and be prepared to open with more energy that you would in normal conversations.
- Maintain this energy and enthusiasm throughout the presentation.
- If people don't know who you are, then your experience and role may be important to them, but also quite boring to listen to. Introduce yourself but keep it brief – people don't need to hear your life story.
- Don't mention the challenges or problems you had in preparing, writing the presentation or arriving that day. Never talk yourself down, for example, 'I am the unlucky one with the graveyard shift sent to bore you this afternoon...'

- What big or interesting question will you be answering? What is the main hook of the presentation? Start with something compelling.
- People quite like to know what you plan to cover, so by all means do this, but again keep this brief with simple, high-level signposts.

General Tips

- You don't need to present a summary of every thought and every step of your journey. Think about the aims of your presentation and keep close to them. Remember, if someone asks you the score in a football match, they are probably not interested in your detailed description of each half, the fans, the ref, the manager or the weather.
- Don't use any notes. Try and get used to your slides being all the notes you need. If you do need a written prompt, have a few bullet points on paper, but don't write things in full and read them.
- Beware of overuse of bullet lists on slides.
- Don't answer questions you don't know. Admitting you don't know can add to your credibility.
- People remember well-crafted stories, so bring your points to life with examples.
- The audience expects your presentation to end with a summary. Make sure you finish with impact and emphasise the key points or the areas you wish them to remember the most.
- Never over-run your time slot, even by a minute.
- Finish slightly early if you can.
- Manage your ending. Don't let the chaos of questions be your close.
- Make sure you look at everyone by scanning the room when you are speaking. Be especially attentive to this when you are asked a question – don't stand in front of lots of people addressing only one of them.

Chapter Summary

1. People assume that your presentation style, content and delivery sums up you as a person. So make sure you present yourself as you would wish to be remembered.
2. Design matters, flow matters, font size matters.
3. Make sure you put some dedicated preparation time into your presentations.
4. Pay attention to your whole environment including the audience, the room, the wider business perspective.
5. Invest in a decent presentation programme that will give you some honest feedback.

FOCUS

This section explores the 'line in the sand' people cross when they move from operational to strategic leadership. A promotion to a senior leadership role carries a whole new set of responsibilities and accountabilities, and the need to take a different perspective. Some people are promoted and act as if nothing has changed. They meet the same people, they go to the same meeting rooms and they get on with their work by immersing themselves into the day-to-day pressures of running a business. What they are missing are the key themes in this section:

Future Orientation: Taking a strategic view of the business. You need to step up to this challenge and work with your team and your peers on how to take the business forward.

Corporate View: Recognising that you are part of the leadership team of the organisation, seeing things from a core leadership perspective and perhaps letting go of some old departmental loyalties.

Clarity: Simplifying the complex and helping people to navigate through difficult choices and challenging times.

Future Orientation

There is no question that working life is busy. Operational pressures abound and it is easy to slip into a reactive and defensive state of mind. This chapter helps you to think through how you may rise above the day-to-day pressures and find the right level of focus for the business.

In my role, I am privileged to work with many senior people. I have found there are two extremes when it comes to focus.

Some managers have a real grasp of the strategic challenge they face. They are able to rise above the minutiae and see the bigger picture. They bring clarity and focus to discussions that provide much-needed direction. However, I also meet managers who wallow in the mire of corporate bureaucracy. You can spot them easily because they constantly complain about having too many emails. They give too much time and attention to peripheral problems, and they engage in too many battles with other departments and functions.

I have divided Focus into three areas:

Future Orientation: The need to develop a strategic view.

Corporate View: The need to see the bigger picture and to see the work of a department or function in the context of the organisation goals.

Clarity: The ability to prioritise and sift information and focus on what really matters.

What do we mean by 'future orientation'?

At work and in life, there are only three areas of discussion. The past and how we got here, the here and now, and the future. The past may be full of memories, stories and experiences, and the here and now may be full of challenges, but we need executives who are able to rise above this and think about the future. The sad truth is that it is incredibly rare for anyone to send a string of emails that say, 'You need to take stock and think about the future of the business.'

Many leaders get caught up in operational problem solving. They respond to emails, share updates, read progress reports and become embroiled in the chaos of the immediate and the here and now. Now, some people reading this will nod in agreement. They will cast their mind to the reality that, while reading this paragraph, a stream of emails will be heading their way. They will argue that other people don't understand the reality of their role and the stress they are under. In other words, it is easy for them to justify the current position. If that is the case, then how come some leaders manage to rise above the day-to-day minutiae and change the scope of their horizons? If you want to develop executive presence, you need to lift your head and start seeing things differently.

I've designed a Business Excellence Model to summarise the challenge all leaders face:

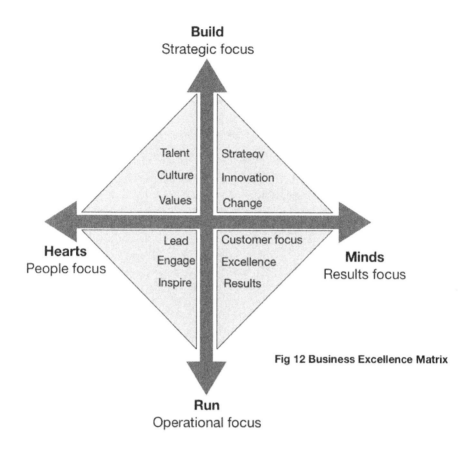

Fig 12 Business Excellence Matrix

The vertical axis represents the time frame of attention. Clearly we need to **run** a business, to make sure it is working well. But equally, leaders need to **build** the business and to help shape its future. This is a delicate balancing act.

The horizontal axis explores whether you focus on **people** and **results**, or **hearts** and **minds**. Any classic book on leadership theory will present a definition of leadership as 'achieving results through people', and this definition is reflected on this continuum.

The model presents us with four potential leadership zones.
Run and Minds (bottom right)

If you are spending time here, you are focussing on operational problem solving. Your attention will tend to be short term and on resolving immediate problems. This section deals with keeping your part of the operation going and trying to improve operational efficiency.

Run and Hearts (bottom left)

Time spent here is all about engaging your people. It covers all the core leadership functions of delegation, coaching, performance reviewing and communicating.

Build and Minds (top right)

Here the focus shifts to the future. This sector is all about business development, product development, innovation and shaping a new business, and how this might be disruptive in the market.

Build and Hearts (top left)

This is the more strategic side of people development where you may focus on organisational culture, values and talent.

The Business Excellence Model provides an excellent summary of the role of the leader. In the context of executive presence, we will use it to make two observations.

If you operate only in the southern hemisphere of the model, you will be perceived as operational and not working at the right level for a more senior appointment. Obviously, you need to spend time in the lower part of the model. The challenge is how often (if ever) you step above the line and work with more strategic challenges.

There is no glory in being a tough manager with a singular focus on results. Equally, work is not a social club that exists merely for the joy of the assembled employees. Both the east and west sides of this model are vital for success, and at the most senior levels in an organisation, you ignore either one at your peril.

Why is future orientation important?

We start our strategic-thinking programmes with Gary Hamel's memorable quote summarising the scope of the challenge:

Somewhere out there is a bullet with your company's name on it.

This really sums up the nature of business and the threat of competition. If you have a successful product or have won a new client contract, the chances are that someone, somewhere is looking in your direction and wondering how they can take your money, your brand, your reputation. This constant pressure leads to only one obvious conclusion:

Trying to stay where you are is as good as going backwards. While you stand still, others are progressing. This means the only option is onwards and upwards.

The challenge for future orientation is not in recognising that it is important, it is in being pro-active and doing something about it. There are a number of clear influencing factors that add to the pressure to become more future oriented.

The speed of change: This is well documented and we recognise that the technology and innovations of today help to create and shape our future. But the pace of change is speeding up, as the technologies themselves help to fast-track the change process.

The expectations of others: The Pareto principle suggests that 80% of the ideas and changes will be generated and inspired by 20% of the people. We can't test the accuracy of that proportion, but we can be clear that people look for role models to inspire them. Many employees expect direction from those in more senior positions. There is a strong link between providing a clear future orientation and motivation. People work harder and more positively if the future makes sense to them.

The Management Team Agenda: As you are promoted within an organisation you will (or should) notice some significant changes to your role. Specifically, you are charged with thinking about the future of the organisation. Reflect for a moment on this diagram:

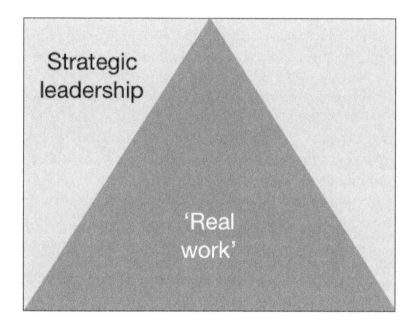

Fig 13 Leadership and 'Real Work'

The labelling is a little tongue in cheek, but it does make the point. At the most junior organisational level, you will tend to serve the customer or get the work done. As your career progresses, your role and function changes. You often spend less time with the customer and are engaged in more time and effort, leading and shaping the future of the business. At least, that's the idea.

What does it look like at best?

Some of the most credible leaders I know have a strong future focus. It is not just what they say themselves, it is the way they engage the people around them in a debate. The best leaders have a complete understanding of the 'run' and 'build' agenda. If you were to be a fly on the wall at one of their meetings, you would notice a defined strategic focus. They would minimise the discussions on admin and car parking. They would close down the meaningless reporting. You would find agenda items that deal specifically with topics such as business development, excellence and raising the bar.

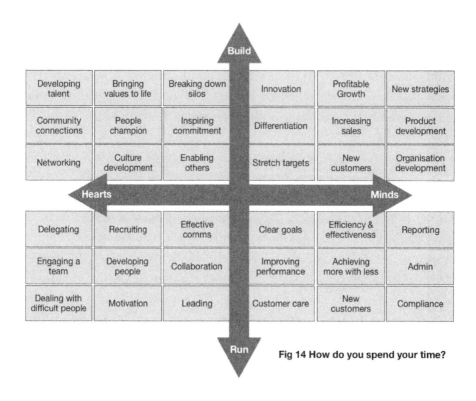

Fig 14 How do you spend your time?

Have a look at the diagram above. We have populated our model with a range of tasks you might associate with the different quadrants. The 'fun test' is for you to look at your last four weeks, and reflect on where you are spending your time. If you venture into the upper half of the model and especially the top right, then you are potentially working at the right level. Spend all of your time on the bottom right quadrant, and you are not.

At its worst

You can usually spot a clear lack of focus at management meetings. It is interesting to reflect that, for many roles, going to meetings is the job. It is what people do. So what happens when you lift the lid on the content and style of poor leadership?

Phil is chairing the monthly meeting. It is held on Floor 7, in a meeting room named after a famous explorer. The air conditioning hums to ensure a pleasant temperature of 21.3 degrees, and the fluorescent lights flicker into life as soon as someone enters the room. Gathered around the table are the six members of Phil's leadership team.

Phil welcomes everyone to the meeting and there are cordial greetings over coffee and custard creams. Everyone settles in for three hours of discussion, and Phil circulates a rough agenda. There are some standard items plus a few other items that have arisen since the last meeting. A calm settles over the room as Phil commences with Item One: a review of the minutes of the last meeting. At this point the team are handed the minutes that have been carefully crafted by Jenny the Executive Assistant. Her written work is exemplary and she has managed to capture an almost verbatim account of the discussion last month. There are four pages of detailed notes. Phil notes with interest that the discussion on this year's budget was left rather open ended and this prompts a debate about who was actually going to do what and when. This is cleared up and, after thirty minutes of discussion, they agree that these minutes do in fact represent a fair and accurate summary of the discussion for last month. The minutes are signed and dated so they can be added to the file of management meetings.

Next on the agenda is the office move. One of the departments is moving to a different floor as a result of a decision to expand the call centre in another part of the building. This prompts forty minutes of discussion around window space, flower pots, water machines and sound proofing. This proves a surprisingly controversial topic that Phil has to stop in the end by suggesting they pick it up again at the next meeting. He thanks everyone for their views.

Next up is an opportunity for each manager to report in with progress and updates. Phil asks Amanda to start with a report from the finance team. Amanda is good at this. She has Gantt charts and slides and pictures and summary papers. Her summary is most intimidating for anyone else in the room, as her report is so comprehensive it implies the four people in her team are each doing a ninety-seven-hour-week on tasks that are critical, not only to her department, but to the survival of the whole organisation. Amanda sits down with a flourish, and Phil thanks her for an excellent summary. He then asks David for his team's report. At the last meeting, David provided a disappointing three-minute summary of his team's progress. David is new and was unaware of what was expected. He has now learned how to shine, so he too is ready with a spectacular update.

And so it goes on. Updates, reporting, office moves, car parking, office parties, budgets, customer problems. At no point does the agenda reach the challenge of the future. There is virtually no place for discussion around future plans, change or innovation.

After three hours, Phil's leadership team leaves the meeting room and Jenny hurries to type up the minutes.

Maybe you have attended meetings like this. At the heart of this rather turgid waste of time lie two critical questions:

1. Does Phil know how to build future focus into his leadership style?
2. Whilst these people are eloquent about what they do all day and how they spend their time, can anyone in the team answer the question 'What are you for?'

How to improve and develop future focus

Helicopter Vision

As a leader you need to rise above the chaos and minutiae of operational problems. This has often been referred to as 'helicopter vision' and the analogy is a good one. It implies the ability to examine the whole terrain from a different perspective. In reality, few helicopters are available on Floor 7 in the Amundsen room. Therefore, leaders need to think differently.
Here are some ideas:

- Create some personal space. You book time for meetings. How about booking some time for yourself?
- Run meetings that only have a future focus. Throw out the 'update and reporting' agenda every couple of months and replace it with something more strategic.
- Change the landscape and tone of the meetings. Try a different location; get out of the building.

Develop a strategy with twenty questions

It is vital to give a clear strategy for your team. Try this test. Ask each member to write down on less than one page what they perceive to be the key priorities for the team as a whole over the coming year. Tell them to summarise what they see as the team's mission. If you receive many different answers, it suggests you haven't invested sufficient time in developing a clear strategy for your team that people can buy into.

My intention is not to turn this book into a manual for strategic thinking, but do have a look at the Strategic Map Model below. This is the framework we use when consulting with senior teams, and it summarises the key areas you need to consider.

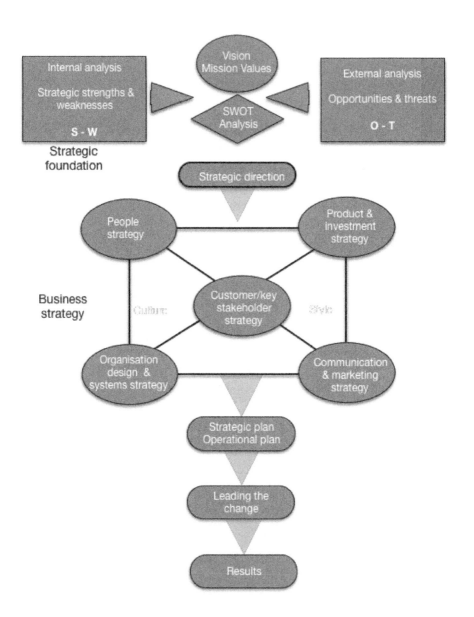

120

The map model prompts the following questions:

1. **Vision**: What is your reason for being at the highest level?
2. **Mission**: Can you summarise the essence of your place in the world in under a page?
3. **Values**: What do you stand for? How should you conduct yourselves?
4. **External changes**: What changes that are out of your area of control or influence are coming your way? Do they represent threats or opportunities?
5. **Strengths and weaknesses**: What are the strategic strengths and weaknesses in your area that make a difference to how you are perceived and what and where you operate?
6. **Strategic direction**: Given the answers to questions 1-5, what are the key priorities for you and your team over the coming twelve to eighteen months?

Questions 1-6 can be labelled as the Strategic Foundation element of strategic thinking. The responses here provide a clear context for the decisions you need to make in the Business Strategy section of the model.

7. **Customer strategy**: Who do you serve and what needs do they have that you must satisfy?
8. **Product and investment strategy**: What products and services will you offer? What new services will you introduce? What should you stop doing? Where do you make the most money or get the highest returns?
9. **Organisation design and systems strategy**: How do you need to organise, structure and manage your part of the business to deliver value to the customer in a way that is efficient, effective and delivers the promise?
10. **Communicating and marketing strategy**: How do you plan to communicate and market your services to your customers and other key stakeholders?

11. **People strategy**: What skills, capabilities and attitudes do you need to develop in your company's employees to deliver your plans?

As you can see, questions 7-11 concern the decisions and actions you will take to bring your strategy to life. But without first thinking through questions 1-5, these are hard to answer.

12. **Financial plans**: What are your budget and your resource plans going forward?
13. **Planning document**: Can you pull together a short summary of your plans as well as a presentation to bring them to life for your wider team?
14. What do you need to do to **lead the change**? What do managers and leaders need to do to make sure everyone is on board?
15. What do you need to do to **embed the changes** you are proposing?
16. How will you **reward and measure progress** against your plans?
17. What will be the **signs of progress** that the plans are working?
18. What **specific results** are you aiming for?
19. Does everyone in your **leadership team** buy into the plan?
20. Does everyone in your wider team understand the **key messages, the key priorities and the spirit** of what you are trying to achieve?

I have framed these twenty questions into the Strategic Map Model, which forms a good summary of the strategic agenda.

Chapter summary

1. You need to develop strong 'helicopter vision'.
2. You will be judged on your ability to rise above the minutiae of the operational and to consider key strategic questions.
3. You need to set the agenda to deal work on future orientation – it is rare for anyone to email you about it.
4. You need to create time to think.
5. You need a strategy.
6. You need to develop and fine-tune your strategic thinking skills. Don't try to bluff this.

Corporate View

What do we mean by 'Corporate View' and why is it important?

There are three key areas within this section and all are important.

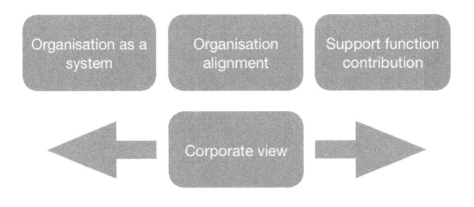

Fig 16 Corporate View

We need to consider the organisation as a system, not individual isolated boxes. The decisions made in one area will have an impact elsewhere, and taking a corporate view means thinking through and working on these connections.

The organisation as a whole will be heading in a certain direction. A key question here is whether your team, your part of the organisation is aligned to the overall direction of the business. What if it's not?

The final and perhaps most controversial element concerns the role of the support functions and how they contribute to the business. To what extent are these seen as adding value and are aligned to the business goals?

The organisation as a system

Here is an easy example to think about. You take some guests to your favourite restaurant, which is as busy as usual on a Saturday night. You are shown to your table and given a familiar menu to peruse. You wait for longer than usual for someone to take your order. Even the drinks are a long time coming. Finally, having ordered a nice selection of food, you sit back and wait for it to arrive. But what started as a pleasant experience now begins to feel wrong. Your guests are great company and are happy to engage in stimulating conversation, but they too begin to notice the long delay for the arrival of any food.

Your level of concern increases to such an extent that you call a waiter to your table to check the progress of your order. He apologises and makes reassuring noises. You are placated, but feel compelled to apologise to your guests and explain that this is not the restaurant's usual standard. In response, they mention some alternative restaurants that 'you really must try and where the service is excellent'. Eventually, the food arrives and it is fine. Well cooked, well presented, and delivered with a flourish and an apology for the delay.

You know the owner pretty well and have a word with him at the end of the evening. He mentions he has reduced the number of waiters in order to save money on wages and increase margins. He apologises for the slow service and is certain standards will pick up again in due course.

This example is an obvious one and something we can all recognise. Intuitively, we can spot a clear connection as follows:

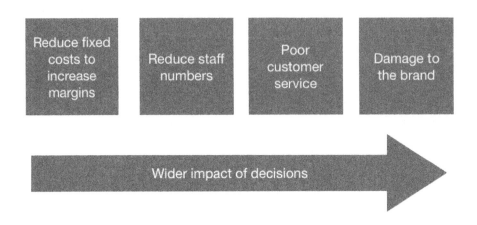

Fig 17 Impact Of Decisions

Taking a corporate view means thinking through the connections and links between decisions. Here are some examples:

What are the costs and implications of saving money?

- If you are choosing to invest time and energy into a particular product, service or innovation, what will you choose not to do? The chances are you can't do it all.
- If you make a decision in your department, which other departments and functions are impacted by this?
- If you increase the pressure to change, in what way could this fuel stronger resistance?
- If you gain approval for additional resource, who is giving up that resource?
- If your project is now the main priority, whose project has slipped down the priority ranking?

Great leaders will map out the connections in organisations, and take a more systemic view of problems and solutions as they work towards finding a solution.

Organisation Alignment

A popular urban myth describes how a visiting president to Space Center Houston asks the cleaner what he does for a living. 'I am helping to put a man on the moon, Mr President,' comes the reply.

This story demonstrates an important principle. No matter who you are in an organisation, you need to show a strong connection and alignment with the highest-level strategic goals. This is true of the cleaner, but even more true for the most senior members of the organisation. I love the challenge that you could ask all the members of a senior leadership team to independently write down the key strategic goals for the organisation, and then compare the list for consistency, connection and alignment.

If, for example, your business is aiming for a low-cost strategy, you need to consider the implications of this before increasing your headcount.

I sometimes encounter senior leaders who do themselves no favours by seemingly rebelling against the strategic direction the company is taking. In a recent example, a leadership team announced a strategy to move 'from good to excellent' as part of a drive for stronger levels of professionalism through the business. The strategy was simple enough. The challenge was to look at everything and see whether it could be improved. There were some who grasped the challenge and ran with it. They set up internal meetings and workshops around excellence, and engaged people in debate and discussions. There were also managers who seemed to resent the initiative. They were too willing to point to the barriers to the initiative. They didn't commit the time to it. They 'played the game' in some meetings but saw the whole thing as an inconvenience that stood in the way of getting the real work done.

Now, I am not advocating blind obedience in the face of corporate stupidity. But if you work for a company that believes in sales or cost cutting or excellence or customer service or market share, be wary of standing against the flow and enthusiasm for that particular strategy. By all means challenge the strategy, after all that's what you are paid for, but once it has been agreed, absorb the key strategic objectives and embrace them. In the worst-case scenario, you can alienate your whole team from the strategic direction of the business. You can also add to the costs and confusion as strategy disappears under a confusion of mixed messages and priorities.

Support function contribution

There is a common activity in corporate life where people divide themselves into those departments that add value and those that add costs. Those who believe they add value love to bait those who they perceive add costs, and they do this at every given opportunity. They love to pick on the HR director or the head of finance for the vast armies of people engaged on the generation of meaningless paperwork, all done in the name of self-justification. Let's face it, they are often an easy target. But let's also consider two key issues here:

1. There is clearly a pressure on all support functions to stand up and be counted. They need to be aware of the first two points in this section and the impact their decisions will have on the wider organisation. They also need to have strong alignment behind the organisation's key goals and strategies.

2. The business needs to be respectful of the contribution the support functions make. Any book on strategy will remind the business that there are a few drivers to a successful business.

a. People are the differentiator and you need to look after them and engage them.
b. All businesses are in part at least an IT company.
c. Get the numbers wrong and you will fail.
d. No great product or service sells itself – marketing is always key.

These four points cover some of the core functions that represent significant reasons for the existence of your support functions. We are wise enough to know that some support functions are poorly run. If you are reading this as a senior player in a support function, then you will understand the pressure. If you are in the 'core business areas', then work with your support functions, rather than against them. At all times, remember you work for the same organisation.

The other matter to raise here is that corporate functions do have some responsibilities that need to be completed for legal or compliance reasons. You may not agree with the time spent on issues like Health and Safety, Data Protection or Employment Legislation, but they are an important part of corporate responsibility. They can also cost your organisation a great deal of money, should you be in breach of them.

Public battles

When you watch a movie about knights in armour, there is a strong possibility that at some point there will be a jousting tournament. Two knights in all their finery, clad in the finest metals, riding the most impressive steeds, with huge lances at the ready. The rules are simple. Ride fast and attempt to knock your opponent off their horse to be claimed champion.

In other words, a metaphor for the argument over the budget or strategic goals. Some managers go to meetings and their strategy seems to be to 'win' and even humiliate the others. There is nothing more satisfying than scoring points off the support functions and knocking them down a peg or two. Some may call this 'corporate banter'; others will call it antagonism. If you find yourself in the middle of a corporate slanging match, remember the following:

- It is always easy to run someone else's business when you are not actually doing it. Management seems easy from the touchline.
- You do work for the same organisation – you are not, in fact, species from different planets. You may see things differently, but the context is the same.
- There is never enough time, resource or money to do everything. Business is always about choices, and discussion is healthy. Battles are not.
- You do have to work together in the morning – your relationships are as important as your work.
- Everyone is watching – you are role models for the organisation. The more senior you become, the more people notice what you do and what you don't do. Your behaviour will be adopted by others. You will influence the culture of the organisation through your deeds and actions.

Tom Peters once said, 'Once a company gets more than ten people on the payroll, it becomes a hopeless bureaucracy.' That may well be true, but few organisations of any size will exist without well-balanced finances, a strong people manifesto and a modern, forward-thinking IT strategy. In other words, choose the corporate battles for finance wisely.

Chapter Summary

1. At senior level, you need to consider the whole organisation in decision making.
2. Organisations are complex systems and your thinking needs to be systemic.
3. There are always improvements and savings to be found inside the system.
4. There are always consequences to the decisions you make.
5. Support functions play a vital part in the success of organisation, so work with them, not against them.

Clarity

And so the great man stood up. He spoke for forty minutes. In that time, he showed eighty-seven slides. He circulated a summary report of 124 pages. He was asked a number of searching questions by members of the audience.

The great man sat down and nobody had a bloody clue what he was on about.

What do we mean by clarity?

A seemingly obvious question, but one that appears to evade many professionals. We have all sat in a room, completely bewildered by presentations and reports. We don't need things to be dumbed down, but we do need them to be clear and this is a real skill. You only have to sit at your desk and look at the sheer volume of emails you receive on a daily basis. Hundreds, if not thousands of them. You will go to an off-site and listen to several presentations, and you will look at hundreds of words on screens. All of this begs two questions that lie at the very core of clarity:

1. How can you sift through the mountains of information and work out what is really important and enables you and your team to progress?
2. How can you make sure that you are clear yourself?

Before we get into the practicalities of clarity and answer these questions, let us firstly consider the work of Thomas Hardy in one his novels, Far From The Madding Crowd. You may have read it, but it does not matter if you haven't. Pick it up from the shelf and you will notice it is a fairly lengthy read. The book itself deals with the trials and tribulations of Bathsheba Everdene and her various love interests. Should she escape with the dashing Sergeant Troy, or settle down with the young farmer-turned-shepherd, Gabriel Oak? Now, the plot is a little more complex than that, but I suggest, armed with that small amount of information, if you were to open a page at random, you would get the idea. You would notice Hardy spends a great deal of time describing Gabriel Oak's habitat. He uses phrases like, 'the dry leaves simmered and boiled in the desolate winds, a tongue of air sending them spinning across the grass', and 'the trees wailed and chaunted to each other in the regular antiphonies of a cathedral choir'. Hardy is famous for his descriptions, and his writing can be a joyful exploration of the English language. He takes a basic idea, like Gabriel walking across a meadow, and explodes it with simile and metaphor. The key point here is that he uses startling vocabulary and a creative imagination to describe the simplest of things. It doesn't matter that we find words we don't understand hidden amongst the descriptions, because we don't lose the meaning. As we lose ourselves to the language, the images, sounds, smells and feelings all come alive in our own imagination.

Now let's compare this with something like A Brief History Of Time: From the Big Bang to Black Holes by Stephen Hawking. Many people bought this book and admittedly many people failed to finish it. But undeniably it is famous for taking some highly complex ideas and presenting them in a way that enabled mere mortals to grasp them.

Imagine for a moment that Hawking had decided to take a leaf out of the Hardy book of writing principles, and had presented his thinking with Hardy's vocabulary. It is doubtful that anyone would have read past a few pages.

There is one other book I would like to reference. Well, not actually a book, but a publisher. I am always impressed by the work of DK publishing. I love the way they pay attention to design, layout connections, simplicity. They are able to present often complex ideas in a way that helps the reader understand them and want to keep reading. Here is a quote from their website:

DK's aim is to inspire, educate and entertain readers of all ages, and everything DK publishes, whether print or digital, embodies the unique DK design approach. DK brings unrivalled clarity to a wide range of topics, with a unique combination of words and pictures, put together to spectacular effect. We have a reputation for innovation in design for both print and digital products.

The following words in particular stand out to me:

- Design
- Unrivalled clarity
- Unique combination of words and pictures
- Spectacular effect

Now let's consolidate the ideas from Hardy, Hawking and DK, and set down the clarity challenge:

Defining clarity

We have four variables as follows:

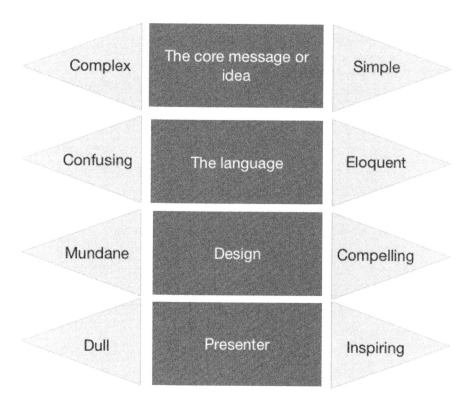

Fig 18 Delivering a Compelling Message

These four variables work in combination, and clearly the first three relate to the written word and overall presentation, while the forth category comes into play when we have a storyteller or presenter to add into the mix.

The left-hand side of the diagram is not ideal. In combination, we have a complex idea that is confusingly written, presented with no flair or imagination, and by some bloke who is droning on and on and on. (Yes, we have all sat through that very presentation.)

In contrast, on the right-hand side we have straightforward ideas that are well reasoned and illustrated with compelling graphics, all presented by someone with flair, energy and enthusiasm.

In the context of executive presence, there are a few home truths you need to grasp about clarity:

- No matter how clever your idea, if you present it badly, people will think it is a bad idea. They are unlikely to support it.
- People are not impressed by technical experts who show off their knowledge.
- People don't need to hear your thinking process and the story of your decision making to feel convinced that you know what you are talking about.
- If you take time to carefully construct your arguments and how you present them, people will be impressed by you.
- The simpler you make things, the more people will trust you.
- People will appreciate and notice the time you have taken to craft something that is designed to engage them.
- If you have ten minutes for a presentation and ten slides or more, you have too many slides.
- No one has time to read a long report.
- Less is more.
- Design matters more than you may think.
- You cannot read font size 12 on a screen from across the room.
- Clarity is seen as a sign of intelligence.
- Punctuation and grammar matter. People will judge your suitability for promotion based in part on your use of commas and apostrophes.
- The ability to be impressive on your feet is a core competence in the boardroom.
- Your ability to communicate through words, sentences, paragraphs and pages is ever more compulsory. If you don't work in a manufacturing role or direct service role, it is likely you will be writing to people and attending meetings. You had better be good at both.

Developing Clarity

Here are some thoughts that will help you bring impressive levels of clarity to the areas you are working on. These notes apply equally to presentations as well as written documents.

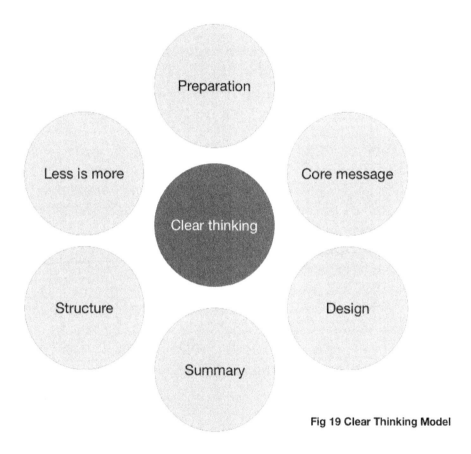

Fig 19 Clear Thinking Model

Preparation

The first point is about giving yourself adequate time to think. Communication is important and you need to prepare for this properly. President Wilson was once asked how long it would take him to prepare a presentation, and he replied:

'It depends. If I am to speak ten minutes, I need a week for preparation; if fifteen minutes, three days; if half an hour, two days; if an hour, I am ready now.'

I don't know if those numbers are correct but I agree, it is important to put some serious preparation time into presentations that require impact, especially the shorter versions. For example, I have been asked to run a lunchtime workshop next week for a couple of hours on why coaching matters in organisations. The session is informal, and I am told to encourage questions and debate. So my preparation time is important, but I will focus on the questions I will ask rather than the things I want to say. Had they asked me to pitch for some work for ten minutes, my preparation and rehearsal time would at least double. So book time in your diary to make sure you collect your thoughts, to shape and structure your thinking, to find some key messages and to draft and refine and rehearse.

When you do your preparation, draft the words and the structure but make sure you allow time and space to encourage honest feedback. All too often when asked for feedback, colleagues have learnt to be polite. This means not being honest that they have been bored rigid by the turgid outpouring of data they have just experienced. You need honest feedback. Work with people you trust and make sure they appreciate that you are trying to craft something impressive, not average.

Core message

Here is the challenge. When you strip out all the detail, what is the one core message in the material and content you are creating? If you have slides, which one slide is the most important? If you are writing a report, what is the key sentence that really matters?

Pinpointing the core message is a great help in providing structure to your preparation. Once you have established your core message, the rest of your material will tend to fall into place. If you can't find the core, you can't identify the one slide that matters, then you may well need to do some more thinking.

Remember that your audience will respect and appreciate clarity. They have only a limited capacity to absorb and remember messages, so make sure your core message is predominant in any presentation or written work.

Less is more

This is clearly linked to the core message paragraph above, but is worthy of some expansion. Imagine that you are giving a presentation and you invite questions. Midway through your presentation, you are asked a question by the finance director. Now, which of these following possibilities is true?

1. She has a genuine lack of understanding or a concern and seeks clarification.
2. She wants to demonstrate that she is on top of the subject and understands it.
3. She is making a point that may be relevant to someone else in the room.
4. She is making a point disguised as a question.
5. She would really love it if you could take her short question as an opportunity for you to open up in detail about your life's work, and deliver a supplementary twenty minutes on the topic.

In truth, it is difficult to know the motive behind a question, but your job is to be respectful of the questioner and to remain brief. No one wants to sit there while you ramble on for eternity.

We are not advocating dumbing down your ideas. The key here is to put hard work into the discipline of summarising your thinking.

Here are a few practical tips:

1. Even the most complex problems, concepts or stories can and should be summarised on one or two sides of A4.

2. Pictures and diagrams are effective at stripping down content.

3. If you are presenting for ten minutes, you should only need between six and ten slides.

4. Slides should be minimal in style. As I mentioned earlier, Seth Godin advocates a maximum of six words per slide. I find it hard to always stick to that, but I remain minimalist in my approach. The last thing people should see is paragraphs and sentences. Your slides should contain the key points at the highest level.

5. Use bullet points and well-thought-through layout to abbreviate your content.

6. Try writing a summary of your topic and restrict yourself to a maximum of fifty words. Once you are happy with the fifty, reduce it again to twenty-five. Then see if you can highlight six key words ... and finally, perhaps, one. This discipline will help you focus on the important issues and messages.

Fig 20 Summarise the Strategy

7. Try crafting an 'elevator pitch' for what you want to say, in which you have only the duration of a short elevator ride to put across the essence of your project to your CEO. Use the following headings to craft it:
   a) The value you hope to bring from the project (the organisation benefits)
   b) The very core of what you are working on
   c) Any specific results or outcomes you hope to achieve

Practise this and try it out on colleagues, aiming to get through the whole thing in under ninety seconds.

The elevator pitch works as long as you are succinct, clear and have thought through the benefits your work will bring.

- When you are asked questions during a presentation, keep your responses brief. If you have more complex thoughts or details you need to get across, do this one-to-one and not in front of a room full of people.

- Don't get tempted to show off how much you know.

- Remember that most people's attention span wanes after fifteen minutes or less, and they get bored reading more than a few pages.

Structure

People who go on presentation skills courses can develop a rather mundane view of structure. They are advised to:

Tell them what you are going to tell them
Tell them
Tell them what you have told them

You may recognise this approach. There is some merit in this structure when we consider the listening patterns of a typical audience member and their attention span:

1. Opening: People wonder who you are and why you are here
2. First points: They wonder what this has to do with them
3. Main points: They want to hear a bit of detail
4. Closing: They are interested in your conclusions and recommendations

We are in part driven by what is known as the Aristotelian method of comprehension. We have learnt that the most important part of a presentation, letter or report comes at the end. If we want to know what a critic thinks of a movie, all we need to do is read the last couple of lines of the review. If you need to know what to do in response to a letter, the last couple of lines will generally contain the call to action. This approach gives rise to a fairly predictable and sound way of structuring a report or presentation.

However, there are other ways to present ideas. Have a look at the following diagram that summarises many components of a report or a presentation, and some short explanations of these:

		Objective		
1	Context	Background	**Situation**	Organisation context
2	Analysis	Consultation	**Perspectives**	External research
3	Evaluation	Disadvantages & negatives	**Options/choices**	Advantages & benefits
4	Call to action	Practical steps	**Proposal/recommendations**	What happens if we don't change?
5	Implication	Support needed	**Results/outcomes**	Organisation impact
		Summary - Conclusion		

Fig 21 Project Structure

Let's explain the model to illustrate constructing a report.

Objectives: Make sure you are clear about the objective for your report. What is it trying to achieve? You will also need to be clear on the objectives for the project you are working on (that may or may not be the same as the first objective).

How this builds credibility

It shows you are focused and helps you to share your goals with others so that they become clear about what you are doing and why. People are impressed that you have been focused and clear.

On the downside

It can be a bit of an obvious (dull) place to start. Many CEOs like to see a summary of the actions and recommendations at the beginning.

Context

Organisational context: What are the key organisational drivers for this project? You might include:

- Company vision, mission and values
- Key strategic goals
- Key priorities
- Recent changes or developments

Background: Why are you working on this? What prompted you to start this work? Where has the initiative come from? What problem are you aiming to solve?

How this builds credibility

This is useful for showing that you are aware of the goals for the business and have written your report with strong alignment to these. It makes your proposals and ideas feel more corporate. A summary of the background also helps people see that you understand the wider picture, the story.

On the downside

You can annoy people by recapping what is well known and has already been discussed at length. If someone gives you a clear brief for a report, they don't need a complete recap to demonstrate that you have listened.

Perspectives

External research and perspectives: Building credibility to your proposals through academic studies, latest research, external data.

How this builds credibility
It shows you are aware of external perspectives and adds weight to your arguments. Research from other organisations or input from other studies shows that you are looking outside your team, your organisation and even your industry.

On the downside

It is possible that external perspectives have only a tenuous link to the problem you are working on. There is also a danger that too much information here makes your work seem more like an academic dissertation and less practical/problem focused.

Consultation: Evidence of who you have consulted in order to develop your findings. How their views have shaped your thinking.

How this builds credibility

It shows that you have done your homework, and demonstrates that you have worked to gain the views and opinions of others, which helps with engagement. This helps you seem more knowledgeable, consultative and connected.

On the downside

People like an expert but they do get bored hearing about detailed research. They need to have confidence that you know what you are talking about without regurgitating every known fact or piece of data.

Presenting feedback from consultation is similar. People like to know that you have consulted, but consultation will tend to generate many opinions and facts. It is up to you to present themes and conclusions, not to summarise every comment and every thought.

Evaluation of options

Advantages and benefits: Presenting the advantages and differentiators to a course of action or option. This will help you gain support/buy-in or, if you are showing the benefits of a less-preferred method, will demonstrate that you are taking a balanced view.

Disadvantages and negatives: Summarising the problems and issues with the options you face. This can also build support for your chosen course of action, or demonstrate credibility in your thinking.

How this builds credibility

Leadership is all about choices, and this shows that you have been balanced and objective in making decisions.

On the downside

You will probably reach a conclusion about your preferred recommendation. We might expect to hear a summary of the strengths and disadvantages of this approach in some detail. We don't need to hear a summary of every possibility or a breakdown of your evaluation process. Certainly, you can keep this in your back pocket to respond to challenges, but no one will thank you for sitting through the history of your decision making.

Call to action

What happens if we don't change? Doing nothing is always an option. In Dickensian terms, you demonstrate the 'Ghost of Christmas Yet to Come', in which Ebenezer Scrooge is shown the implications of carrying on his existing lifestyle. In business terms, you show the likely outcome of carrying on as you are.

Practical steps: The decisions and actions you recommend, and the key action points.

How this builds credibility

In business, people want practical outcomes, and want to hear the end points. Clarity here suggests that you are action oriented and able to translate high-level project plans into tangible, clear deliverables.

On the downside

Too many reports end with a recommendation for more research. Conducting further investigation and analysis may in some cases be a good move, but all too often this is a way of proposing an extended deadline. You also need to be clear with your proposed outcomes, which means summarising data into tables and highlighting the key deliverables. Pages of recommendations are often as unclear as submitting many pages of analysis.

Implication

Organisation Impact: Outline of the implications of your proposals on the wider organisation.

Support needed: The resource, time and other support required from other people to bring your proposals to life.

How this builds credibility

It shows that you have put your project into a wider organisational context and presents you as more of a systems thinker. It is rare for a project to have no impact on other departments or functions, and a summary here shows a broad understanding of the organisation. It also demonstrates that you appreciate (need) the positive contribution of others to get things done.

On the downside

Many people are 'copied in' on information, often because the sender likes to see themselves or their function as at the heart of any project. But the more people you involve, the more layers of potential bureaucracy you are likely to trigger. Be aware that involving others is time consuming and may not help get the work done.

Summary & Conclusions: A recap of your proposals.

How this builds credibility

People like to see a crisp summary and conclusion. They are likely to pay special attention to this and clarity here shows respect for their time.

On the downside

Strong opinions and firm views can be abrasive. If your report is thorough and your recommendations are unequivocal, then you have earned the right to be firm. Beware of emphatic recommendations on the back of spurious or inadequate research.

Building clarity by thinking through structure and content

This approach is not designed to capture every element of a written report or presentation, but it does contain many of the key themes you could potentially include. One thing is for certain: if you include everything in detail, those on the receiving end of your written report or presentation are in for a long session.

Some tips on structure:

1. Think about the needs of your audience. Give them what they need.
2. Beware of too much background information.
3. It can be a good idea to start with your conclusions.
4. You don't need to present the story of your thinking process. It is the conclusions and insights that are interesting.
5. Stories work – people are intrigued by them. Starting with a session on what happens if you don't change can be engaging. Painting a visual picture of an interesting future can also be compelling.
6. Let the narrative flow – consider storyboarding your ideas before you start writing the detail.
7. Signpost things for people. Make sure your headings are clear.
8. It is nice to surprise people with your structure.

Focussing on the things that matter

The final point on clarity concerns the very real skill of being able to focus on what matters most. The best executives are able to sift through information, and not waste time on less important things.

Here are a couple of tests that can help you to achieve progress in the right areas.

Connection with the strategy: After many years of not winning any races at all, Ben Hunt-Davis and the GB Men's Rowing Eight won gold at the Sydney Olympics in 2000. They changed the way they worked, which changed their results. One of the key learnings from this time was a decision they made to subject every element of their preparation to a simple challenge. For each element they asked, 'If we do this, Will It Make The Boat Go Faster?' (the title of Ben's book). This challenge and attention to detail produced a real focus on results and improvements.

This criteria is something every manager can adopt. As a manager, you may not be rowing for Olympic gold, but you will have some clear organisation goals, strategies and ambitions. As you prepare to share a report or arrange a meeting, ask yourself: Will this make the boat go faster?

In addition, you may find this matrix a useful tool:

Make a note of all the things you have to do and evaluate them according to the following two criteria, using a scale of 1-10.

1. If you achieve this, how much will this move us towards our business goals?
2. How easy or difficult is this? For 'difficult', think through the complexity of the work, the costs and the time involved.

This will help you to review the challenges in front of you.

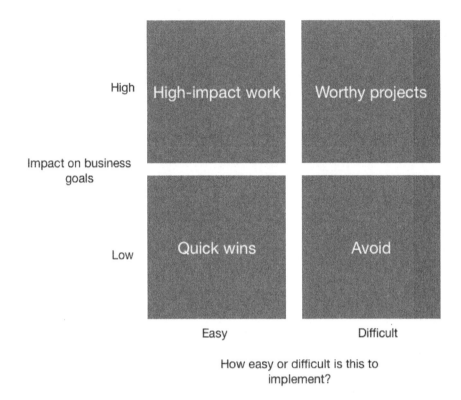

Fig 22 Idea Selection Matrix

Quick wins: These are simple things that won't make a huge difference individually, but they all add up. Remember that excellence often comes from many small changes. It is critical that you get these off the table quickly and don't spend too much time implementing them. They are supposed to be 'quick' wins.

Avoid: If you do a lot of work here, then you need to challenge it. For example, if you have a huge and apparently meaningless report to do, then trace the source of it. Take the person who needs it out for coffee and talk to them. Do your best to get rid of this drain on your time, or at least to minimise it.

Worthy projects: You need to find time to schedule the worthy and more complex projects. These are the things that often get squeezed out through day-to-day operational pressure.

High-impact work: This area is clearly a high priority. It has a significant impact on your ability to meet your goals, is quick or demands little time and resource. Make sure you do these and don't let the monotonous admin take over.

Chapter summary

1. Less is more.
2. Work hard at design and simplification.
3. You need to have a strategy, and everyone needs to know what this is.
4. Your strategy should shape and define how you spend your time and what is important.
5. You need to think wider than your own team, your own department. Networks and connections are everywhere.

EGO STATE

You are about to walk into a difficult meeting. The stakes are high and all eyes are on you. As you take your place at the table, how do you feel?

The Executive Presence Model contains many key areas, but perhaps none more important than the Ego State section. Ego State contains three areas that have a powerful influence over how people approach their role and the impact they have.

Within Ego State we explore the following:

Passion: The level of optimism, enthusiasm and positivity.

State management: Levels of self-control, especially during times of great stress or pressure.

Self-belief: Personal belief in the ability to perform the role at the highest level.

So what comes first? Do you need to have strong self-belief to be impressive in the role? Or can you grow into the role and develop self-belief over time?

I believe that self-belief, experience, reflection and feedback are all important. In a recent coaching assignment, I was chatting to a senior leader who had just been given an executive role. There was no doubt that her confidence and self-assured manner at interview stage helped win her the job. During our coaching conversation, she posed the question, 'What happens if they find out that I am not as confident as I appear?'

This is a common concern for senior leaders. They are in a role with many significant challenges and may have little support from their boss, who expects them to be self-sufficient. They feel the pressure to demonstrate confidence in the role. They also need to cope with the toughest of days with style.

The following sections are not intended to replicate a self-help book, but we will work through some of the key areas I explore through executive coaching.

Passion

Where do you encounter negative people? You meet them in reception on the way into work on a Monday morning. You find them in meetings, sitting on the furthest chair from the front. You find them hidden in the responses to the emails you send out. They wander into your office for a quick word. But the worst place to find them is when you look in the mirror and discover a permanent frown that has been furrowed through years of worry, sarcasm and negativity.

Here are some familiar words and phrases that indicate you are in the presence of misery...

- 'Fine thanks, it will soon be Friday.'
- 'I think you will find we tried that in 1863, and it proved unsuccessful then.'
- 'We have always done it that way.'
- 'Sorry, that's not my role.'
- 'Thanks for letting me know, but I already knew that.'
- 'I remember the days before the merger when we wouldn't have done this sort of thing.'
- 'That may be acceptable for a training course, but welcome to the real world.'
- 'Bloody management – couldn't run a bath.'

Radiators and drains

In a massive simplification, we divide people into two categories. Some people are **radiators**. It feels good to stand next to them, especially on cold days. They radiate energy, positivity and warmth.

Some people are **drains**. They sap your energy and erode your enthusiasm. You would rather not stand next to them, and if they suggest a beer after work, you make excuses. When you spot them in a meeting room, you quickly head towards someone else.

If you happen to get caught next to a 'drain' you will spot something in their language. They will use negative language; they will use the word 'but' more than is helpful; they will sigh with indifference; they will laugh sarcastically; they will tend to ask fewer questions and make more critical observations.

What we are looking for are people with enthusiasm. If you have interviewed people for a job or sat through a presentation recently, enthusiasm is a wonderful engagement tool.

I had the pleasure of listening to Richard Branson talk about his life as leader of the Virgin brand and what defined him and his success. He was incredibly humble and had a few simple observations.

Positivity: Richard surrounds himself with positive people. He admitted that if he entered a room and heard people complaining and badmouthing others, he would rather leave the room. He confessed to having perhaps naive optimism about the future.

His recommendation was to not spend time on the draining things – he couldn't see the point in working on things that didn't excite you personally. I guess that's easy to say if you are a multi-millionaire, but think about your own job, the challenges you face. If you are not excited about that, then it will show. The work will suffer and so will you.

Recruitment: When asked what he looked for in colleagues, Richard explained he places great emphasis on those who have the capacity to connect with others. He looks for warmth and for people you feel you would like to work with.

No mistakes: It was interesting to hear Richard describe the experience of trying to win the contract to run the UK lottery and his subsequent battle with Camelot (the competition), the British government and the legal system. He lost this one despite a great deal of personal effort. In his own words, he quickly moved on from this failure. It was a good idea, they worked hard and it didn't work out, and so he moved on to the next challenge. So when you think about your failed ambitions, the lost job opportunities, the rejected pitches, the real question is this: how much effort do you spend running over the failure, examining it, trying to understand it, justifying it, worrying about it? Perhaps your energy is best used elsewhere.

When I coach someone, it is interesting to ask them about the career choices they face and how this model comes into play:

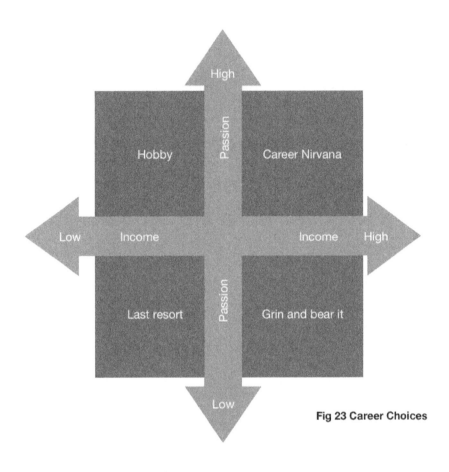

Fig 23 Career Choices

This compares two key variables in career choice: how much you earn compared to how much you love your job.

Last Resort: This is a job that pays poorly and doesn't engage you. We call it the last resort, as it is a means to an end. It pays the bills, at least some of them. You do this because you have to. Someone who has been made redundant and needs to keep up the mortgage payments may end up here. The recent graduate who is still trying to break into their chosen career may well be here, waiting tables while looking for opportunities to follow their dreams. If you find yourself here, you need to remain positive and put on a brave face. This is not where you want to be, but your mindset is still critical.

Hobby: This is typically low paid (sometimes not paid at all), but you do it because you love it. So if you spend time working with a community group or put on productions with a local theatre, you do so because it energises you and fuels your need to connect with people, to be part of something. The rewards here are not financial but personal, developmental, perhaps spiritual and make you feel good. If you are involved with a group of people who get together outside work, whether it is a band, a theatre company, a scouts group or a book club, at the heart of this is someone with a passion to get things moving, surrounded by people who are turned on and tuned in to that purpose and that ideal.

Grin and bear it: This is the toughest box on the grid. Here the pay is good (at least good enough), but the work doesn't excite you. It can be pretty depressing to encounter people who live their life in this box. They don't like what they do or the people they work with. When they think about coming to work, they are prone to spontaneous sighing. Engage them in conversation and they will complain and challenge new thinking. They are unlikely to be the best leader, the best at customer service, the best engineer or the best sales person, because their lack of engagement and commitment will leak into everyday behaviour. When you hate your job, it is hard to fake excellence. Customers can see through any facade you present.

With leadership, a lack of passion shows even more, as a team will recognise a leader who is merely going through the motions every day. If you have ever worked for a boss who is fed up with the organisation and their place in it, you will feel their discontent with every meeting. They are inclined to complain more and defend more. They will often try and recruit more team members into their club – a unique band who join together to moan about the business. They are miserable and want you on their side.

Career Nirvana: This quadrant is for people who love what they do and get paid well for it. They can be overheard telling people that every day is a joy. Many journalists, musicians and actors are here (especially the famous ones), but many business people are too. I coach people who love their job and their company. They come to work each day fired up and feeding off the challenges that each new day brings.

So the question is, where are you?

From a coaching perspective, my most challenging clients are those in the 'grin and bear it' box. Well-paid executives who dislike what they do every day is a tough challenge. I say tough, because financially, this box is okay. I know people who are far from retirement but are hanging on for the pension they will be guaranteed with a few more years' service. Others admit that they are well paid but figure they are unemployable anywhere else, so resign themselves to hanging on.

This quadrant has worrying implications for executive presence, as you are likely to be building a reputation for negativity. Your 'legend' will be tarnished by stories of you being difficult, argumentative or just plain boring. The longer you stay in this box, the worse it gets. I remember meeting a guy called Peter early in my career. He was clearly bored at work and spent his day avoiding doing anything challenging. He would sidestep responsibility, and would read newspapers at his desk for as long as he felt he could get away with it. He was quick to criticise and always looking for collaborators to join in, as he mocked the ambitions and plans of the organisation. I noticed his style on Day One and asked someone about it. I was told he had behaved this way for twenty-three years!

If you go shopping for a new bed, the advice is always to buy the best you can afford, as you spend a lot of time in it. Surely a job presents a similar situation. Is it too much to suggest that your quest should be to find a role that engages you, challenges you, excites you?

I do understand that you can't always shape the organisation. However, chances are that if you are reading this, you are at a senior level or at least aspire to be there. It's likely there is no clear job description for what you do. No competency model has been written to nail the skills you need to do your job. The parameters that surround what you do and how to do it are flimsy at best. In other words, your role can be shaped, moulded, changed and adapted. Perhaps there is a way for you to feel better about it.

For people who lack passion, it is easy to suggest 'Well, go get some, then,' but the reality can be somewhat difficult.

The following list of recommendations for if you find yourself in the 'grin and bear it' category is not exhaustive. But if you lack passion for work, then I have some suggestions for you.

1. Recognise it. Acknowledge how you feel on a Sunday night with work looming on the Monday morning. Perhaps you need to wake up to the fact that if you don't enjoy your job but have chosen to stay put, it is likely to impact your performance and how people perceive you.

2. Stop moaning to colleagues. There are thousands of jobs in the world, and whether you like it or not, you decided to take the current role. You are also choosing to stay there. If you hate your job and you choose to stay there, then at least stop complaining about it. Take responsibility for your decisions.

3. Be careful about how much you complain to friends and family. People who are miserable at work often go home and take their frustrations out on those closest to them. Beware of doing this day in, day out. You will become unbearable to live with.

4. Ask more questions. Engage with people. Explore more, be curious.

5. Turn up your listening. Be interested in other people and what they have to say.

6. Say 'Yes' more. There is an amusing book by Danny Wallace called Yes Man, in which Danny resolves to spend a whole year saying yes to everything. As a result of this approach, he experiences many strange events, goes to odd places and meets new people. The chapter on work makes for fascinating reading. Danny starts to say yes a lot more at work. His job at the BBC expands in synchrony, and his approach opens many connections and opportunities. People who lack passion often stop being involved in things. They turn down opportunities and keep their heads down. Perhaps it is time to say yes more than you say no.

7. Try things. If you have kids, you will know the challenge of getting them to try a new food. As their taste buds develop, they can become set in their ways and resistant to new flavours. If you ask them to try something new, they will screw up their noses and decide they don't like it before they try it. Then, as the food reaches their mouth, they respond by spitting it out, proving they were right all along. Is it possible to see the same behaviour in adults? Of course it is. I ran a seminar recently for senior leaders and asked for a show of hands. I wanted to know how many of the group were active users of Twitter. The group concerned was a typical fifty-something audience. What was interesting was the number of hands that went up as non-Twitterers. What was more interesting was how disparaging so many of them were about it. They were quick to condemn how trivial it was, how superficial, how irrelevant. One element in particular defined their response: ignorance.

None of them had a Twitter handle; none had tried it; none had explored it. People say they hate opera without ever going to one. They hate ballet without seeing it. The same is true at work.

8. Choose one day – perhaps tomorrow or a day next week – and resolve to remain positive for the duration. See how you get on. In other words, don't think about changing your attitude for the rest of your life, but get your head around a single day of positivity. You need to do this by using the techniques explored in the Legend chapter and by projecting how you want people to think, feel, say and do as a result of meeting you.

Chapter summary

1. Bring your energies to work, as this will infect others.
2. Be a radiator, not a drain.
3. Try things; be an enthusiast for the new and the novel. Be especially wary of condemning anything you have never experienced.
4. Be wary of going on about 'the old days' and living with memories. Make today memorable.
5. Don't remain in a job you hate unless you really have no choice. It is better for everyone that you are in a role and environment that brings out the best in you.

State Management

Imagine you are up to your neck in water. The water level is rising and heading towards your mouth, your nose. How do you react? Do you panic, or are you able to remain calm?

You are at a management meeting and someone is openly critical of the work you and your team have been doing. How do you react?

Imagine you walk into the office and spend a couple of minutes with each person at a time when everyone is under pressure. You meet high performers as well as those struggling. How do you behave?

You have heard that your team are making errors, and customers have begun to notice and to complain. How do you approach your team? What face do you present to those who work with you?

The above questions all raise the issue of 'state management', which inevitably becomes a more significant issue the more pressure you feel. This book can't calm you down or manage your behaviour for you, but the following points may help.

Controlling your own anger and frustration

Simon is a senior leader within a well-known manufacturing and engineering company. I was asked to coach him as part of his development plan, following a grievance that was taken out by a member of staff against him.

Simon is a well-meaning and all-round nice guy. If you met him, you would enjoy a beer with him. You would imagine him to be a good boss. But he had one significant problem. Simon had a very poor performer working for him, and one day Simon lost his temper. He shouted at the member of staff in full view of their colleagues. His team member complained about his behaviour, and it was Simon who ended up in front of a disciplinary committee.

When I first met Simon, he was fuming. He described his staff member's track record of poor performance, insubordination and, in Simon's words, 'taking the piss'. When he described the events leading up to the incident, I could see why he was angry. Indeed, in some companies, his behaviour would have gone unpunished. But, as I told him at the time, it is okay to say you are angry but not okay to be angry. Deep down, Simon knew this. In my time as a coach and facilitator I have experienced some jaw-dropping behaviours by managers against staff. (A quick hello to Tony, who remains proud of throwing a colleague through the partition wall.)

Here is a straightforward view of state management:

You should never, ever lose self-control.

The very second you do, you stop appearing as a leader and lose the respect of those around you.

Losing your temper is one of a number of behaviours that has the potential to destroy your reputation and your gravitas.

Perhaps you can understand why Simon was emotional. You may reflect on a number of moments in your own career when you have felt emotional. The key question here is what do you do with the anger, the emotion? To start with, you need to notice and acknowledge your own emotional state. If you feel yourself getting angry, then pay special attention to how you behave, how you are seen. You can't control instant emotions, but you can control how you react to them. Remember this formula:

Event ⊢ Reaction = Result

You cannot usually change the event. There was little Simon could have done to prevent the actions of his staff member, but he could have managed his reaction. Had he done that, he would have maintained his professional credibility.

Create some space for yourself: When you feel emotional, take yourself away for a while. Never speak while emotional or angry at work. Never fire off an impulsive email; always sleep on a tough response.

Talk things through: When you feel emotional, it can help to talk about it. If you have a difficult member of staff, talk to someone in HR. If you have a coach, talk to them. Sharing the problem will bring different perspectives and will lead to a calmer response.

Notice your own emotional state: Have you noticed when you become visibly frustrated, bad tempered or emotional? If you reflect for a moment, it is common for us to be emotional with others when we feel under pressure ourselves. For example, it is common for parents to be less forgiving with their children after a bad day at the office. There may well be a correlation between how you talk to other people and your own state of emotional well-being. It might serve you well to remind yourself of how you are feeling and whether you are being harsher than usual with those around you.

Put things into perspective: Here is a story I use in coaching. Imagine you are decorating your living room and are painting the ceiling with white paint. You are standing on a ladder in the furthest corner of the room, when you notice a hairline fracture in the plaster. It is noticeable close up, and you are faced with a simple choice. You can get down from the ladder, find some plaster and fill the crack, allow it to dry and then sand it and paint it. Or you can quickly add some surplus paint to your brush and hope to cover it up without doing too much work on it. You choose the latter. A couple of days later when admiring your work, your eyes are drawn to this corner. You can't help but notice the crack. For you, it becomes the focus of the room. When friends pop round for drinks, they are in the middle of praising your decorating skills when you interrupt and point out your shoddy handiwork – something they would never have noticed otherwise. This story serves to remind us to put our own and other people's errors and mistakes into perspective. It is rare to have a member of staff who is a complete disaster.

Look for the motive: If you work with someone who is disruptive, ask yourself why they are behaving like this. What is the root cause of their behaviour? It is rare for someone to come to work purely to appear vindictive or disruptive. If there is one common denominator in human behaviour, it is that people behave in a way that they perceive will present themselves in a good light. Few employees come to work just to surround themselves with anguish and chaos, with the main aim of making themselves look bad. So if you encounter behaviour that makes you react in a negative way, search for the root cause. If you can understand their motives, perhaps you can better control your reactions to their behaviour.

Beware of the assumptions that drive your emotions: Imagine this. You are a member of a theatre group that meets for rehearsals every week on a Tuesday evening. You arrive one Tuesday to find that several cast members arranged another rehearsal the previous Thursday without telling you. You are upset by this, as you have been a member of the group since the beginning. Here is the internal story you create as a result:

- They probably met at one of their houses.
- No doubt they had food and wine as well as rehearsed.

- They had fun and there was a lot of laughter.
- They probably discussed you and your role in the play, and whether you had the right part in the next production.
- This is probably the first in a number of rehearsals taking place without your involvement.
- This is probably the beginning of the end of your leading role in the theatre club.

Perhaps this is something of an extreme reaction, but you get the idea: A simple event happens and you extrapolate it and make assumptions. The weird thing is that the assumptions make you mad, not the event itself. So next time you find yourself extrapolating, ask yourself whether it is the event that is causing you to feel upset or the assumptions you are making about it. We often create our own misery.

Behaviours to break

As you progress through your career, you will pick up a range of behaviours and traits along the way. Some will be from training programmes or coaching. Some will be habits you pick up from other leaders and professionals. You will observe their behaviours and adopt them into your own style. You will also retain a range of behavioural traits that have been with you since your schooldays. Some of your approaches you will put down to your personality. In other words, your current style and approach has been formed from life experience. I am sure a psychologist could deconstruct you and identify the precise moments from which a behaviour or approach became part of you, part of your behavioural DNA.

This book isn't able to dig that deeply into your psyche, but I have observed a number of behaviours and traits that I believe are destroyers of executive presence, and would like to share them with you.

Before we explore these, consider the following statement.

I can't help behaving the way I do. I am [insert nationality, religion, gender, etc] and that's just the kind of people we are. There is nothing I can do about it.

To what extent do you agree with this? Is your behaviour fixed and there is nothing you can do about it? Are all New Yorkers brash? Are all northerners blunt and to the point? Are all Londoners too busy to connect? I am not talking about how we label or stereotype others, but how we label ourselves. What behaviours do you hold that you attribute to a particular view of yourself? This question is important, as it raises a key area. To what extent do you think you can change how you behave, and how fixed are the habits that define you at work?

Below I have listed the most common behaviours I observe through coaching that need to be eradicated. As you read through this list, think about your own approach and whether you are guilty of some of these.

1. Bad listening

We have covered some of the core listening skills in our Social Skills chapter, but poor listening is a common trait and something to work on. Sometimes there are giveaway signs that prove you are not listening. One of my colleagues has the habit of checking his watch mid-conversation, almost as a reminder that he has something better to do.

2. Competing for dominance

I met an old friend and it was great to catch up with him. He told me about an Eric Clapton concert he had attended. He said he had enjoyed it a lot and I was immediately reminded of my own experience seeing the musician. It was on a beautiful summer's day in Hyde Park in the presence of Prince Charles and with the legend that is Steve Gadd on drums. Yes, I may have won this bout of 'See who has had the best experience of seeing Eric Clapton', but can you see what I did there? I managed to take my friend's experience and turned it into a competition, which I won, thereby undermining and deflating my friend.

You may not be discussing guitar heroes, but perhaps you are discussing projects, problems, challenges. The challenge here is to recognise to what extent do you listen and to what extent do you see conversations as mini competitions. Why couldn't I have just said something like, 'Oh, I love Eric Clapton too, what did he play?' In other words, I replace my competitiveness with curiosity.

3. Using your phone during meetings

I have mentioned this elsewhere in the book, but it is worth reiterating this point here. Constantly checking your phone sends an unmistakable signal that the people who are not in the room are more important to you than the ones who are. Show your respect for your present colleagues by leaving your phone out of sight for the duration.

4. Condemning your own team

Here are a couple of examples for you to reflect on:

I was coaching someone recently and she drew a structure chart, demonstrating how she was at the top of a typical hierarchy of people. As she worked through the list, she pointed to a couple of names, describing them as 'hopeless and a lost cause'.

Back in the days when I worked in corporate life, I recall taking a phone call from a senior leader in the business. They called to complain about a course they had been on and challenged the quality of the training, specifically the credibility of the trainer. The course was on time management and apparently, my colleague had spent the first hour doing 'mindless introductory exercises that had no place in the corporate world, but perhaps a place in a nursery school'. It was a tough call to receive.

How should you respond to these examples? What do you say to the manager who condemns her own people? What do you say when someone criticises your team with good reason?

These questions get to the heart of what we might call 'corporate responsibility'. Or, putting it another way:

'If you condemn your team, you condemn yourself.'

If you think about it, you recruit someone, you train them, you agree their objectives and you unleash their talents on the business world. If they screw up, where have you gone wrong? Now it may be that you have inherited some poor-quality people who are underperforming. Well, my accusation remains: what are you doing about it?

It isn't acceptable to complain about your team as if you were blameless. These are your people, and you are coloured by the perception other people have of them. Our motto for leadership is that you should:

'Surround yourself with brilliance.'

If you don't have brilliant people around you, at least work on it. And never, ever complain about your own team in public.

5. Being late

Many people complain about meetings. They say, 'The trouble with my day is that I have so many meetings,' whilst not realising that going to meetings is the work. That is what they do for most of the day.

I run many workshops and am most amused by the excuses people come up with for late arrival. The favourite is to blame the traffic: 'The M25 was busy,' they say, or 'There was a delay on the Tube'. I have now perfected my 'Oh, that's such rotten luck' response, and wonder if they detect the heavy sarcasm in my reply. Ideally, I would like to add something like, 'Wow, the M25 was busy? Who would have thought it!'

I once had a coaching client take a photo of the chaos at Waterloo to prove that her late arrival was not her fault. Which was ironic, since her coach had passed through the very same station unhindered ... an hour earlier.

The issue of tardiness brings the following consequences:

- The psychology
- The impact

Let's start with the psychology. Being late is a mindset, not a traffic problem. Okay, I agree that once in a while the forces of nature will conspire to close all the roads, cancel the trains and block all the entrances. But these moments are rare.

Here is the challenge:

Imagine I were to put a large pile of money on the table – £500,000 in notes – and tell you it was yours for the taking. It will be there between 9:55 and 10:00 a.m. next Tuesday in an office near Liverpool Street. The money is yours: all you need to do is turn up at that time and you can have it. However, at 10:01 the money will be taken away and the opportunity will be lost. The question here is: would you be there on time?

For most people, this is a no-brainer. Of course they would. They would probably stay the night in a nearby hotel and be there early the next day. In other words, if it is important enough, you make the effort. By the way, when I run workshops in London that start at 10:00, I stay over the night before. Our clients are that pile of money. I have a two-hour commute, and I refuse to run the gauntlet of the transport system. I will never ring in with an excuse to participants on a training programme.

People often blame chaotic diaries for appointments that are rammed together. They complain of meetings overrunning. They leave too little time between meetings. They talk about their diary as if someone else is in control and appointments are out of their hands. The cure to lateness is not to blame your personality, the traffic, other people or your diary, but to resolve to sort it. You need to be accountable for your own timekeeping and you need to start now. Try the next seven days and see how you get on. See if you can manage your time so that, over the next seven days, you are always on time.

Perhaps you are still not convinced, and for that we need you to be aware of the impact of poor timekeeping. Here are some examples to show why lateness destroys executive presence:

Signals

The board meeting starts at 9:00 a.m. and you are late for it. What signal do you think this sends to your colleagues, your team, your boss? The word 'disrespectful' should spring to mind, along with the words 'low priority'. Being late suggests you have better things to do. One of my favourite CEOs was from my days in financial services. He was wholly unforgiving of people late to the boardroom. At the start time of the meeting, he would ask for all the unoccupied chairs to be moved away from the table. Anyone late would then be faced with organising their own furniture, much to their embarrassment. He would also refuse to acknowledge the latecomer's arrival. He would not recap the meeting, nor would he greet them. You would only be late once.

Being calm and in control

I was running a strategic off-site in Wembley Stadium. If you have been there, you may recall Wembley Way, the long walk from the train station to the stadium. You may also recall the flights of stairs and escalators that raise you from the FA main entrance to the concourse where the meeting rooms are located. It may also interest you to know that most of the meeting rooms are right around the other side of the pitch. In other words, this is a long walk. Or a long run, as in this case. Imagine the scene of the manager who has found the M25 to be unseasonably busy and the Tube trains unforgiving. His late arrival at Wembley Park eats at his professional conscience and, as the doors open, he decides to make a run for it. He rushes along Wembley Way, panicking as he passes closed hot-dog stands. Out of breath, he finally reaches the FA main entrance and hurriedly searches for his meeting details. He takes the escalator steps two at a time, and half runs, half walks the circumference of the Wembley pitch. On arrival at the right door, he bursts into a conference room. The room is full of professional people, all seated. They all stare at him and then look away. He mutters an apology and searches for a seat. He finds one in possibly the worst location in the room and sits down. Dishevelled, hot and bothered, he then spends several minutes looking for papers and wondering what is going on. He needs water but the glasses and jugs are out of reach. A stress-induced headache begins just behind his right eye and he finds it hard to concentrate, even when settled and eventually, hydrated.

Now ask yourself, is this a man you will trust with big decisions for your business? If he arrives like this for a strategic off-site, how do you think he will behave with customers and clients? In other words, we extrapolate meaning from this chaotic-yet-isolated scene, and begin to doubt his professional credibility. We wonder if he runs his personal life in the same manner.

Time to think

When I run a coaching session, I allow ten minutes before the session starts to focus my attention. The meetings are important, and I won't be on the phone when my client arrives. I won't be late for them. I will be ready. My papers will be in order, and I will greet my client with professional calm. Those few minutes get me into the mindset for the session. What do you notice about your own landing, your own readiness for the meetings you have arranged or the ones you attend? Are you 'in the zone', or is your attention elsewhere?

Disrespectful

I was running a workshop where the participants were presenting their ideas for strategy and change to three of the board members from their company. The meeting was due to start at 9:30, and John, the operations director, was keen to start on time. At 9:45, one of the participants arrived and quickly made excuses about a meeting that had overrun. John stopped the meeting and asked who he had been meeting that had delayed his arrival. The participant blustered his way through an apology. John then announced with an almost musketeer level of flourish that he had an early meeting with the CEO, but had cut it short in order to be on time for these presentations. He had told the CEO of the company that he had to leave because he didn't want to let the participants down. He then suggested that if the delegate was late again, then he shouldn't bother to come along to the training at all. The public nature of this dressing down was somewhat shocking, but I had to applaud the sentiment. Someone senior had shut down a meeting with the CEO in order to honour a commitment. This raises one of the crimes against leadership. How often are you late starting meetings with your own team and use the excuse that more senior meetings have over-ran? Think about the signals this sends out. You may wax lyrical about empowerment, but what you are really saying is, 'Sorry I am late, but I was with the really important people and I would rather let you down than them.' Do that often enough and the message is pretty clear.

6. Saying one thing and doing another

The expression 'walk the talk' is perhaps overused, but you can destroy your reputation by inconsiderate behaviours that fly in the face of what you (apparently) stand for.

Linda was a senior manager and believed in empowerment and staff engagement. She wanted people to feel important and part of her team. In one example of saying one thing and doing another, Linda had an interesting approach to train travel. If travelling with a junior colleague to a meeting, she would meet them at the station, buy two different classes of train tickets, and would then trot off to the first-class section alone, agreeing to meet her colleague on the platform at the other end of the journey. Words fail me!

7. Forgetting your view of the world

Imagine a pilot and co-pilot flying a passenger aircraft. They sit in a sealed-off part of the plane with all the dials, the charts and the data. They have a nice, clear windscreen so they can see where they are going, and they are in control of the throttle and the levers that determine altitude, speed and direction. They have headphones and clipboards, and are in constant contact with air traffic control and with each other.

Compare this with the view from the seats at the back of the plane. There the field of vision extends to the seat in front, the occasional small screen and a safety briefing. There is a marked difference between the levels of information, the degree of control between those in the cockpit and those in the seats. For example, supposing the people in the cockpit learn of the need to divert the flight due to severe weather in their planned destination. The pilot and co-pilot will have a detailed conversation about this; they will be in touch with air traffic control and will be the ones to change the flight path. Those in the back have a very different experience. The changes are announced and that's about it.

Much has been written about communication in organisations. Everyone agrees it is important but, all too often, senior people forget that not everyone experiences the organisation as they do. Equally, those at the back of the plane don't get the chance to process the decision or to feel part of it, which means they are far more likely to be resistant when announcements are finally made over the tannoy.

The key behavioural message for leaders, therefore, is to get out of the cockpit, to connect with the people and not to remain stuck in the office. In their book In Search of Excellence, Tom Peters and Robert H. Waterman Jr introduced us to the term 'Managing By Wandering Around' – a direct plea to senior managers to stop hiding in their offices and to connect with their people. In Up The Organisation, Robert Townsend suggested that CEOs should, on promotion, have their office taken away and be given a space by the photocopier. This would force them to wander amongst the employees and do a lot of listening. The complaint from the team and those around them should be not that 'they never tell you anything', but rather that they are constantly chatting.

8. Going on about the old days

I worked with a guy called Steve who would often refer to his previous role. He would speak with great affection about how the team worked, the products and services they provided and the attitude to customers. There is nothing particularly wrong with that, except that he worked there nineteen years ago. He talked about it as if it were yesterday and would drop comparisons into every meeting and at every opportunity. I am not going to condemn his past, as clearly Steve had some strong and affectionate memories of it. But I do challenge the inference that the story of the past will bear relevance to today's business challenges. So much has moved on that the environment, the technology and the people will bear little resemblance to today's situation. Please don't think I don't value experience, but I worry that old stories are pulled into the modern world and presented as a potential panacea for all problems. It's a bit like picking up an old business book and reading case studies of companies that have long since gone out of business. One of my favourite Tom Peters quotes I picked up at a seminar (and he may have been quoting someone else) was:

'He doesn't have twenty-five years' experience, but one year of experience he has repeated twenty-five times.'

How true that is for many people.

9. Black Hat Thinking

Edward De Bono published some impressive research on creative thinking, and came up with the idea that there were six thinking hats we might wear during a discussion. We won't replicate the research here, but two particular hats are relevant to this section. De Bono observed that, when presented with a new idea, we might wear one of the following. The yellow hat is a hat of optimism, and looks for all the good in the idea. The black hat is more critical, and looks for problems with the idea. De Bono is clear that both hats are useful in a discussion.

Our observation is that constantly wearing a black hat will erode executive presence. The black hat wearer will only see problems, and will be critical, perhaps cynical. On my training programmes, I ask participants to mimic the sound made by a mechanic who looks at your car or the heating engineer who looks at your boiler. There is often a long intake of breath and a shake of the head, as they prepare you for the sad news they have to tell you and the costs you are about to incur. Some managers are like that. One of my coaching clients confessed to starting every sentence with the words, 'Let me tell you why that won't work'. Every proposition is met with resistance, every concept met with a challenge. Many people will, of course, argue that these challenges are essential as we improve things. Indeed, we need people to question ideas and to challenge our thinking.

Unfortunately, some people never take the hat off. They wear it every day and often seem to revel in their own reputation for cynicism.

10) Praise, thanks and recognition

In one of my early jobs, I worked with an older woman called Joyce. I was only young and it seemed she had worked for the organisation for at least seventy years (okay, perhaps not seventy years, but definitely a long time). Joyce was in a mid-level manager role and was one of those people who seemed to know everyone and everything. Sadly, Joyce was also very negative. She had the ability to find things wrong with everything, and working with her was hard. She was quick to be critical, and you never knew if she was happy. I once heard an anecdote that struck a chord with me that described life with Joyce.

If you have been to a bowling alley, you can picture the scene. Ten pins in the distance, a heavy bowling ball gripped between a thumb and two fingers, and a large scoreboard above your head. You take aim, release the ball and watch as the pins tumble. If you get a 'strike' and all the pins fall over, the animated screen bursts into life and a cut screen celebrates your achievement. The goal is clear and the results are immediately obvious.

With that in mind, let's imagine Joyce running the bowling alley. She would take away the scoreboard. She would be the one keeping score. She would put a large sheet halfway along the bowling alley so that you could no longer see the pins at the other end. She would then put her chair and her desk by the pins and shout instructions for you to bowl. So you would walk to the alley, pick up a ball and throw it to the best of your ability down a pretty much blind alley. You would see the ball disappear through the curtain, and you would hear some noise, but without really knowing what had happened. Every so often, Joyce would emerge from behind the curtain, wearing a disappointed frown and announcing 'you missed four'.

And that was working with Joyce. She saw it as her role to dish out criticism and I can hardly remember a smile or word of encouragement.

There is an interesting end to the Joyce story. She was a few days away from retirement, and I was in the office when a letter arrived from her from the Chief Executive. He wished her well in her retirement and listed many things he valued about her, giving personal thanks for her contribution. This was no standard letter; it was carefully crafted and mentioned many projects Joyce had worked on over the years. Joyce put down the letter and looked quite emotional. I asked her what was up and she showed me the letter. I said something like, 'Wow, that's terrific, Joyce, what a nice note to get.' She replied, 'I am really surprised, because I didn't think he knew who I was.' And then it hit me. Joyce had worked hard for the business for years but had never received any praise or recognition herself. The CEO left it until a few days before her last day to say thanks and that he appreciated everything she had done.

In that moment, I realised that Joyce was treating others as she had been treated herself, and there was far too little colour, fun or praise in her working life.

If you take a moment to reflect, I bet you can remember all the moments in your career when you have been surprised by a moment of praise.

As an executive or senior leader, you will see things going well. Sometimes the people working hard will not be on your immediate radar, so seek them out. Ask your team for support and do something in person to say thanks. Not an email – they are too fast and too impersonal. Make a visit, buy some wine, make it public and don't keep praise to yourself.

Changing our behaviours

We have described some of the behaviours we observe as destroyers of executive credibility. So with these in mind, here is a short checklist of the behaviours that build it:

- Practice your listening skills - pay attention - be curious
- Revel in other people's stories - don't compete with your own
- Put your phone away during meetings and encourage others to do the same
- Always support your team in public - take personal responsibility
- Be on time all the time
- Be a role model - be consistent and respectful
- Be ab obsessive communicator and remember that people don't share your view from the cockpit
- Live in the present and don't clutter meetings with old stories
- Say yes more - look for the good in ideas
- Praise people and make an effort to give personal thanks and feedback
-

Reacting to decisions that don't go your way

I was chatting to an executive called Andy, who had seen a company through some dark times. The business had been through two significant mergers in the space of five years, which had put a great deal of pressure on the management structure. I asked him how he coped with the challenges that inevitably surfaced during such upheaval. This conversation gave rise to what I refer to as 'The Decision Model' that has become a regular feature in my training programmes and coaching sessions.

Andy described the difficult world he faced as part of an executive team. The mergers forced big decisions and short time frames, with many people paying attention to the outcomes. He was also aware that he wasn't the only member of the team during this time. The executive team had grown with newly arrived members, each of them intelligent and forthright. They had to agree how to merge whole departments, which IT system to use, which HR system to adopt, which products to focus on, whether to keep satellite offices open and so on. I asked him how he coped in the middle of this environment with so much change.

He told me that the trick was to make sure he was part of the debate. He saw it as his responsibility to contribute to the decisions that would shape the future of the company. He also confessed that one of the key issues for him was to recognise when a decision had been made. He explained that it was easy for someone in the management team to keep going back to something that had already been decided. People have a tendency to challenge what is already a done deal. He described this as the need to 'spot the moment when the decision has landed and your contribution turns from constructive support to negative criticism.' How true that is. In the early stages of a debate, our discussion and challenges are helpful, but as soon as the decision is made, we need to shift our attention to the question of how to implement the decision, not to carry on challenging it.

In another example, consider a situation that will be familiar to many – applying for an internal promotion and not getting the job. Imagine that your boss resigns and the job is advertised. You are one of three direct reports to the vacant role and all three of you apply. You do your best at interview, and at the end of the process it is announced that the role has been given to an external candidate. Now the three direct reports have a choice about how to react.

Choice one: This person **resigns**. They were hoping this role would be the springboard for their career but it wasn't, so they will find a role elsewhere.

Choice two: This person quickly gets over their disappointment and resolves to **support** the new manager. They get on with their own job and work hard to help the new manager to settle quickly.

Choice three: This person is bitterly upset by the decision. They feel the decision not to give them the role is a poor one and they let everyone know this. They **complain** to those close to them, they imply the process was unfair and when they go home, they complain there as well. When the new person starts work, they smile on the surface but deep down they look for opportunities to trip them up. They undermine them when they can and are difficult and resistant during meetings.

Our three disappointed candidates demonstrate the three reactions that are common for any decision that doesn't go your way. To what extent do you support it and make it work? If you disagree that strongly, is it something that would compel you to resign? Or do you transfer your negative energy to others and spend all day, every day complaining about the decision?

Here is the decision model as a diagram that shows the flow of the process and the options open.

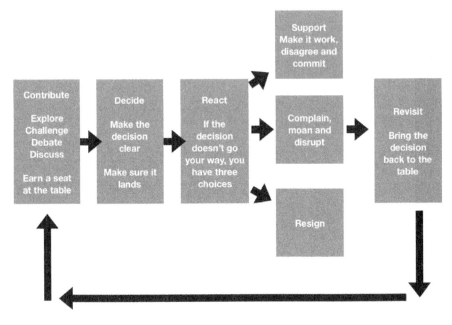

Fig 24 Decision Model

Contribute and be part of the debate

If you are a senior leader, you are paid more than your junior colleagues. This is where you earn your money. You need to recognise that your role is to contribute to and engage with the discussions. If you have 'a place at the table', then be present and add your talent and intellect to the discussions. You need to accept that you won't always be involved in key decisions. In large and complex organisations there are times when you are involved and times when you are not. To quote the great Bruce Hornsby, 'That's just the way it is'.

When A Decision Is Made

Make sure you are clear and other people are clear, and play your part in communicating this. You have a responsibility to help bring the decision to life. It is common for decisions to be made and for people to carry on working and debating something well past the point of no return. So play your part in making sure the decision lands well.

Your Reaction

Consider your reaction when decisions are made that you don't agree with:

a) Support: If you don't agree with a decision but nevertheless it is made, then the challenge for you is to show positive leadership. I picked up an expression used in the Intel Corporation, which is 'I disagree and I commit'. A straightforward challenge to your emotions and your preference, and a defining moment. The moment when you have had your say, a decision has been made and now you need to support it and make it happen.

b) Complain: People with low executive presence often reside here. They carry on complaining about a decision long after it has been made. In the worst-case scenarios, they try to disrupt or sabotage the chances of the decision being successful. We classify this as a 'red card offence' for leaders.

c) Resign: If you are faced with a decision that you don't agree with, then you have the option to leave the business. As an example, if you are overlooked for promotion you might decide to look for a job elsewhere. We find some executives struggle when the direction or values of the business they work for stops matching their own. For example, if you work for a manufacturer who decides to employ child labour as part of the production process, you might rebel against this and hand in your notice.

d) Revisit: I added this box to the model to recognise that, if you disagree with a decision vehemently, you do have the option to challenge it at any time. This box represents the choice you make where, instead of supporting or implementing it, you decide to put the debate back onto the table and to explore it some more. In the model, this is represented by a couple of arrows, but the reality is more difficult, as well you know. You need to have the time, the influence, the energy and the business case to review a decision.

e) Time: I haven't put a box called 'time' on the chart, but clearly all decisions take time to be made, time to land and time to implement. If your organisation makes a decision that you personally don't agree with, then time will normally bring bad ideas to the surface. You need to do your best to help the decision to succeed. Sometimes organisations make mistakes and, if that is the case, then the decision and the consequences of it will inevitably come back to the table at some point. Sometimes you just have to wait.

Chapter Summary

1. People look to senior leaders for signs of confidence. If you appear in control, people feel better.
2. When a fireman walks into a burning building, they do it calmly and use their training and experience to guide them. They don't run around like a headless chicken. You need to bring that same sense of calm to work.
3. Sometimes decisions won't go your way, and how you respond is critical. You will waste a lot of energy attacking a 'done deal' in the organisation. Sometimes you need to disagree and commit.
4. In a senior role, you have access to much more information, data and insight than other people in the organisation. They look to you to be a role model, for clarity and communication. Remember, they don't start with your level of knowledge and buy-in.
5. Be respectful and kind in the way you deal with others. It goes a long way.

Self-Belief

The connection between self-belief and achievement has been well documented. I was reading some statistics on football teams and success only this weekend, and found this quote through The Sunday Times 'Think Tank' (the guys who crunch data to analyse the football scores):

'A team with confidence that exceeds their actual ability can win games that, on paper, they have no right to win. As soon as they recognise and accept the reality of their lower abilities, they start to lose.'

Certainly, when it comes to nouns like 'presence' or 'gravitas', people often connect them to adjectives like 'confident' or 'self-assured'. It is hard to see someone as having presence when they look nervous, scared, uncertain or chaotic. To explore this topic further, let's pose a couple of assumptions and see how they stack up.

Assumption 1: You develop self-belief by investing time and energy into improving your craft

Assume you are an actor and you need to go on stage. The play you are about to perform is Rosencrantz and Guildenstern are Dead by Tom Stoppard, which contains a great deal of fast-paced wordplay and dialogue. Reading the play on the page is enough to make anyone nervous, so to combat this you spend hours and hours learning your lines. Once learnt, you meet with your fellow performers and practise the banter until the lines sit intuitively on your tongue. On opening night you have some minor butterflies, but deep down inside, you know you have this nailed. You walk onto the stage and deliver an impressive performance. There is no question that without learning your lines, you would have felt incredibly nervous in the wings. You would probably have fluffed many of the lines.

There is some old footage of Frederick Herzberg (whose research into motivation created the Motivation-Hygiene theory) presenting to some students. Frederick mentions he was walking through the lobby of a hotel and saw a grand piano in the corner. But, he announces, he didn't feel like playing it that day and invites the students to guess why. They shout out a few suggestions such as, 'You were too busy,' or, 'It was too public,' and so on, until one of them offers the correct reason: 'You can't play the piano.'

And there we have it: Frederick didn't feel like playing the piano because he didn't know how. This anecdote demonstrates the very real connection between skills and motivation. We are rarely motivated to do things that are outside our comfort zone or area of capability. There is no question, then, that to cultivate credibility at the most senior level in an organisation, you need to develop skills and capabilities that will serve you well in the boardroom. You can't exist on bravado alone; you are likely to be found out.

I was coaching a senior leader working as a new member of the executive team, and I asked him how it was going. He admitted being nervous about an upcoming strategy meeting where he was expected to deliver a draft strategic plan on behalf of his business division. I suggested he bring his initial thoughts to one of our coaching sessions, so that we could work on this together. He arrived with some notes and thoughts that were, frankly, dreadful. His work on the plan was haphazard at best, and his draft presentation contained nothing but assumptions and platitudes. In the session, he confessed he didn't know how to draft a strategy. He had never done this before, but didn't want to ask anyone in case he looked stupid.

Some readers may remember the Peter principle (developed by Laurence J Peter), in which the original principle states: 'In a hierarchically structured administration, people tend to be promoted up to their 'level of incompetence'. My client, I feared, had been promoted to a level of incompetence. He may have moved from an operational role to a strategic one, but his skillset remained the same. He had a senior title and a position at the boardroom table, but not the skills and capabilities the role demanded.

This case reminds us that working at a senior or executive level places increased demand on capabilities such as problem solving, decision making and employee engagement. Sadly, you can't put a stack of management textbooks under your pillow and come out full of the knowledge and skills you need after a good night's sleep. Like an actor learning lines, you need to put some effort in.

Assumption 2: If you fake confidence, you appear confident and become confident

Perhaps contradicting Assumption 1 is the idea that you can fake confidence and you will be seen as confident. I spent an enjoyable evening with Steve McDermott, the author of How To Be A Complete And Utter Failure in Life, Work & Everything, which, despite the title, contains many pearls of wisdom around the psychology of achievement. I remember one key mantra from Steve that has stayed with me: 'Fake it till you make it,' he said. 'Get your head around a success mindset, and you will become successful.'

I put this idea to the test when I enrolled on a fire-walking seminar, where the challenge was to walk barefoot over hot coals. There are many views about how or why fire-walking does or does not burn you. But there is one thing I can promise. If I were to put a pile of burning embers in front of you and suggest you put your foot on it, you may well consider me insane. The very idea is crazy, never mind how or why it burns your feet. So the question is, how do they get you to do it? In the case of my seminar, the answer was most definitely practice and getting your head around it. We spent an afternoon practising the walk. We practised how we would walk up to the coals, how we would feel as we stood there and how we would walk across. We even practised the celebration afterwards. The session was intensive and by the time I did it for real, I felt ready. My mind was clear; I knew how to do this. I focussed on getting on with the task at hand and there was no doubt that when the instructor said 'go', I would stride across the coals.

Now, it is pretty rare to walk over actual hot coals in an office but they become a metaphor for awkward meetings, difficult discussions and challenging presentations. I have come to appreciate that Steve is right. You can fake it and, if you do, your mind sends signals to your body that create a positive outcome. In terms of executive presence, this is important.

I remember coaching a deputy headteacher who had been given the feedback that she lacked executive presence. After a few minutes in her company, I could see why. Her mindset was all wrong. She was nervous about attending management meetings and spent time fussing over tea and biscuits for everyone. When I talked through what was going on for her, she confessed to feeling something of an outsider in the group. She was recently promoted and felt uncomfortable taking her seat at the table. She went through a strict assessment centre to get the role and, as far as I could see, had all the necessary skills and attributes to perform at a high level. Yet her problem was that she walked in with the confidence levels you might expect from a supply teacher, not a deputy head.

Assumption 3: Your inner voice matters

I am often amused by managers of lower league football teams whose squads are about to face Premier League opposition. A microphone is put into the face of the manager as part of the pre-match ritual and he says something like, 'We are really looking forward to the game and the lads are full of confidence.' Is that truth or bravado speaking? Are the lads really full of confidence?

When studying human behaviour, we learn that what people say and what people think are not the same thing at all. For example, our parents teach us to lie to our relatives and tell them we loved the Christmas jumper they bought us (even though it is hideous). We call this being 'polite'.

At work, there is pressure to sound in charge, confident and calm. As an example, if I meet a fellow consultant and ask them how things are going, I am always met by a response that suggests they are flitting from one Fortune 500 company to another on a daily basis. No one admits their fears, worries or concerns.

In my study of executive presence, I have found that self-talk does matter. What people think about has a habit of leaking into their behaviour.

If you have ever prepared a presentation, a speech for a wedding or a complicated negotiation, you may hear yourself saying things like, 'You had better not screw this up.' Your head becomes full of your biggest fears, and guess what? In all the confusion of the moment, you are indeed more likely to 'screw things up'.

So imagine this. You are about to jump out of a light aircraft on your first solo parachute jump. You are 3,000 feet in the air and naturally nervous. The parachute instructor makes plenty of reassuring noises but talks about where you might land. He tells you that you are over open ground, and there is clear terrain for miles. Just make sure you don't land on the old barn.

As you jump out of the plane, what do you think of first? The answer is the inevitable, 'Where is the barn?' Followed by this inner dialogue:

Where is the barn?
I can't see the barn.
Damn, the barn is out there somewhere. I wonder if it is under me.
I don't think I could cope with landing on the roof...
Oh my God, I can see the barn. I can, in fact, see the barn.
Jesus. I am drifting towards it. It must be the wind.
If I can just pull down on the left toggle, I think I can avoid the barn.
Damn, this is close. I still might hit the barn.
Here we go, here we go. I am landing!
Phew, just missed the barn.

Perhaps the barn story is a daft example, but it illustrates an important point. Having been forewarned about the barn, the only way to avoid it was to find it. Thus the voice in the parachute jumper's head pulled him towards the one thing he needed to avoid. How true is it in life that we become our worst fears? The person who stands up to present with an inner voice repeating 'I must not forget my words' is likely to follow that very command.

Assumption 4: Failure is a learning process, not proof of inability

In the consultancy business, we often have to tender for work. It is part of the life we have chosen, so we end up writing proposals and going along to presentations. Sometimes it is good news and we win the work; sometimes we don't. The worst cases are the ones we don't win, and we find we have been wasting our time. I can remember being given the opportunity to get some detailed feedback on a failed bid. Price-wise our company's bid was fine, and the quality of our proposal was excellent. Our approach was great, the client liked us a lot. In fact, we had everything going for us apart from one thing. The company that won the work had an account manager who was close friends with the decision maker.

Now, we could complain all we liked about the process and the decision itself, but there was nothing we could do about it. However, this case does generate four key questions:

1. How do you respond to failure?
2. What can you learn from it?
3. How much time do you invest in going over the failure in your mind or in discussions? Is there a point where you are wasting your breath and your energy?
4. How does failure impact your self-esteem and your belief in yourself and your mission in life?

The key here is to put failure into context. If you have a growth mindset and believe in your own potential, then it is so much easier to package failure as part of the experimental and learning process. If, on the other hand, you have a pessimistic view of your own potential, you can perceive failure as proof of your deep-seated fear of inadequacy.

Assumption 5: Self-confidence is a spiral

Intuitively, we know the model here is true:

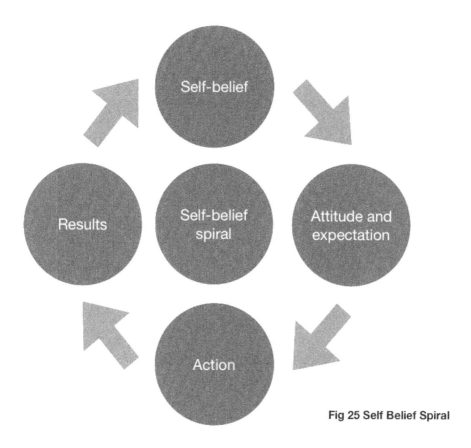

Fig 25 Self Belief Spiral

Levels of self-belief fuel our attitude. Our attitude determines the action we take, which then produces a result. This in turn fuels our self-belief and thus we create a self-belief spiral.

You can see this work with a fifty-three-year-old manager who has been made redundant. The redundancy hits the core of her self-esteem; her mindset is negative. She believes she is unemployable. As a result, she applies for few jobs and gives a poor account of herself in any interviews she attends. The panels think she sounds rather sad and desperate, and give the jobs to other applicants. This all adds up to the proof (as she defines it) that she is unemployable.

The opposite is also true. Someone full of confidence is able to cope with rejection and move on because, deep down, they have belief in themselves.

This spiral is true for executive presence and perhaps forges a link to the previous assumptions. Those with a strong belief in their abilities to work at the most senior levels in an organisation will feel confident in their role. They will have a positive mindset and are unlikely to be phased by awkward people, big decisions or difficult moments. Their action will be positive and they will behave in a way that seems confident and assured. This will fuel positive outcomes in terms of results and the feedback they receive from others. This in turn fuels a stronger sense of self-belief.

Developing self-belief

If only there were a pill to take or a potion to drink that would transform the under-confident to the ranks of the authentically self-assured. Sadly, no such pill exists but there are some points you can work on.

Develop your craft

You need to learn the skills and behaviours that will serve you well in the boardroom. To help you think this through, here is a list of skills and competencies I believe are the bedrock of excellence at this level. This table doesn't cover everything in a senior leader's toolkit, but I have focussed on the areas that define credibility in the boardroom.

	Key Development Areas
Strategic thinking	The role of the senior leader - Building a competitive business - Best practice in strategic thinking - The context for strategic thinking - External and internal analysis
Strategic planning	Strategic planning frameworks - How to construct vision, mission and values - How to pull together a strategic plan - Strategic planning tools and techniques
Excellence	Excellence and what this takes - How companies can go from good to great - How to engage people on a journey - Building a sustainable business
Customer focus	Best practice in strategic marketing - How to identify attractive markets - Differentiation strategies - The impact of price and value on customer behaviour - Building a service-oriented culture
Results focus	How to build a performance-based culture - Performance management schemes; what works and what doesn't - Becoming results focused
Change orientation	How to develop a culture for change to become the norm - Culture change and how organisations form and develop - Handling resistance -How to start a change movement
Emotional intelligence	The psychology of achievement - Coaching skills - Listening skills - Strong self-awareness Influencing skills
Know the numbers	Key numbers - Key ratios - Building a successful business

As explained above, our table doesn't cover every eventuality. I can remember coaching a CEO who came to a session with an idea for the acquisition of a competitor. Our list doesn't cover the skills involved in that challenge. Nor does it cover how to deal with union reps who are threatening to walk out over a pay deal. Such is the complexity of the role in the boardroom, and a comprehensive competency model would fill far too many pages to be worth reading. But this list is a good place to start, as it contains many of the core skills that build presence and credibility. And, we should add, get the job done.

Our list also assumes that you have a strong grasp of basic (core leadership) programmes.

So here is what to do with it:

- Review each area and consider whether you believe this is a core skill for you.

- Read the detail. In my view, these key skills and competencies are too important for you to dismiss them and think 'someone else in the team has this covered'.

- Identify the key areas of need for you and develop a personal development plan to start increasing your skill set.

- Be selfish with your own development. It is common for senior people to lose sight of their own development through being busy.

- Find some learning programmes that are pitched at board level. If you go on external programmes, make sure you are rubbing shoulders with people who hold similar jobs.

- Consider bringing someone into your organisation to work with your whole team.

- Engage with your L&D specialists in the business – they may have access to resource or connections.

- Put some budget aside for your own development.

- Be wary of dismissing any areas on the list. You may feel apathetic when you read words like 'develop emotional intelligence', but the skill set in every area is important. Don't allow your personal preferences, likes or dislikes to get in the way of your learning. In fact, I would be so bold as to suggest that the more you rebel against one of the items on the list, the more you probably need it.

- Use the list to think about developing the talent around you. Who is your potential successor and how ready are they?

The other point to make around developing your craft is to be constantly hungry for learning. Take all the opportunities you can for learning, networking and connecting. Remember, you are developing those vital piano-playing skills. There is a strong connection between your skill set, your motivation, your actions and your credibility.

Practise the look and feel of confidence

I have referred to this previously, but the 'fake it till you make it' principle applies here. I was impressed by a head of department of one of the large banks who told me about his ritual before his most high-pressure meetings. I have used that to produce this list of practices that can help to build your perceptions of self-confidence. Some of the items here may sound trivial, but when you add them up, they work.

- Get a good night's sleep.
- Get up early and arrive early.
- Polish your shoes.
- Make sure your hair looks good.
- Make sure your clothes are professional, clean and pressed.
- Don't let the traffic worry you and stress your arrival time.
- Allow time before and between meetings to get mentally prepared.
- Don't check your phone before important meetings – don't even look at it.
- Don't smoke anywhere near the boardroom.
- Beware of drinking on duty. The two don't mix well.
- Pay attention to your posture – stand tall, keep your head up.
- Greet people with a handshake and a smile.
- Don't try to show off or impress people with your stories. You are more impressive when you listen to theirs.

- Be aware of how you are breathing. Take a few deep breaths before you say anything. Slowing your breathing may help slow your tendency to gabble.
- Don't complain about your journey or the weather.
- Practise your brave face – if it is a tough day, you mustn't look hassled.
- Summarise what you hear more than input new information.
- Use the techniques described in the Legend chapter to make your desired impact.

Controlling the inner voice

When coaching people, I pay particular attention to their language. When they have a significant challenge coming up or an important moment, I ask them why they have raised it.

Here is an example of a recent response to a question on a staff off-site:

'I am running an off-site next month. I have my whole team there and I am worried that it will be boring. The last one was a bit dull, and I am concerned that this one could go the same way.'

This sentence is loaded with negativity. The following diagram shows the link between these negative self-talk patterns and how the voices in your head can create the reality. Your self-talk impacts how you behave and how you act. Those around you tend to pick up on this and behave accordingly.

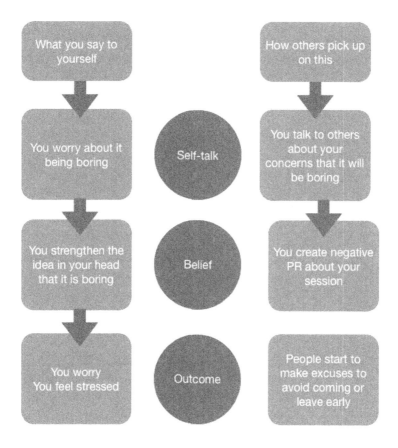

Fig 26 Negative Self-talk and Outcomes

The issue of calming negative self-talk is a considerable topic in itself. The following are simple techniques to get you started:

- Notice when you do it. If you find yourself thinking things that don't actually make logical sense, then it is likely to be an example of self-talk in action.

- Be especially careful of the language you use with others. If you worry that a meeting will be boring, talk to people about how you can make it more energising rather than

205

'How can we make the meeting less boring.' In other words, don't speak your self-talk out loud. If you are worried about making a fool of yourself at a meeting, think about how you can make a positive impression instead.

- When you are about to go into an important meeting, be mentally prepared. Imagine a positive outcome, with people nodding and smiling in agreement.

- I suggest you read The Chimp Paradox by Professor Steve Peters – one of the best books I have read on the power and impact of self-talk. Professor Peters uses the metaphor of a chimp inside your head that is often emotional and irrational. His research contains some sound words of wisdom on how to manage the inner chimp – read it and absorb it.

- Remember times when you were on form and performing well. If something is worrying you, bring to mind a moment when you were feeling confident. Recall that moment and bring it to life in your mind. Adopt the posture and the mindset of success and being positive.

- Talk things through. The negative words and ideas in your head are perfect topics for conversation. Find a good coach or a mentor you trust, and spend time exploring the issues. Avoid people who just dish out reassurances like, 'Don't worry about it, you'll be fine.' They mean well, but their advice is mostly useless.

- Avoid things or people that make you miserable and that make the negative self-talk even worse.

Failure as learning

If you can recall your childhood science lessons, you may remember that science is based on trial, error and learning in order to progress thinking. I remember getting a chemistry set as a kid and trying to make something that smelt awful or would burn or explode impressively. So I mixed things in tubes. Some experiments worked and some didn't. I learnt from my mistakes.

I remember designing some early training programmes for teams and leaders. I wanted to help people learn to become great leaders and/or great team members, but I also wanted them to enjoy the learning experience, so my course design was based around fun, insights and success. I gave people a few models to think about, and set some team and leadership challenges that were mostly within their grasp. The programmes were energetic and people liked them.

My own view of learning changed when I went to a training programme designed by the Leadership Trust. The Leadership in Management residential course involved being put into a team of seven people for five days and being given a succession of challenges. The challenges were complex and demanding. My team failed for three days solid. We were bad at everything. We ran out of time, we failed to communicate, we didn't read the objectives properly, we made incorrect assumptions and our nominated leaders were conspicuous by their absence. I can remember one of the facilitators coming out and announcing that the teams on our programme were among the worst he had seen.

The programme is based around a classic experiential learning cycle like this (see overleaf):

Fig 27 Experiential Learning Cycle

The course gave our team a wealth of experiences that contained many moments of failure, forcing us into ever more detailed reviews of our performance. Out of that came some powerful learning.

Now, I am not advocating that you spend your life experiencing monumental failure in order to keep learning. But here are a few thoughts that should live with you on this topic:

1. If you are doing anything interesting, you will fail. It is inevitable. A marketing project will fail to deliver; a product won't sell; you won't get a job.

2. You need to learn from it. Spend proper time and energy digging under the detail of the failure. Be honest, explore it and extract every nugget of improvement you can from beneath the surface.

3. Don't dwell on failure for too long or beat yourself up over it. You can invest too much time and energy in things that are not working, and there is a time to draw a line under them and move on.

4. Be careful of the standards you expect of others. This is especially true the more senior you become. I have heard many leaders quote the phrase 'Get It Right First Time' and attempt to live by this mantra. That is a sizeable demand on people who are trying new ideas. I am not sure any successful product has ever been developed to be 'right first time'. So celebrate failure and attempts to succeed as much as you celebrate success.

5. Try again! There is no doubt that persistence pays off. But also beware of what we call the 'low-beam syndrome'. That's where you live in a house with low roof struts and one of them has a sign that says 'Mind your head', yet you keep bumping into it. Don't expect a different answer if you keep doing the same thing over and over again. Become adept at trialling things, exploring, testing, prototyping.

Appreciate the Self-Belief Spiral

The spiral has many uses but let's focus on the aspiration to develop executive presence. Most people can acknowledge the connection between self-perception and performance.

Key to your success at a senior level is your level of self-belief. When you consider walking into a boardroom, how do you feel? As I am writing this, I am on the way to a meeting with a large European Bank, where eight senior people will evaluate my proposal for senior leader development. I can't predict what they will say or know what they will think. But I am sure of a number of things:

Equals: I will walk into the room with an equality mindset. I don't see the panel as superior beings; I consider them equals and we are coming together to share some thoughts and swap ideas.

Expertise: I know my stuff. I am not proposing anything outside my area of expertise. I have put many thousands of hours into developing my craft, and I am confident to handle questions and diversions. I also know enough to admit that I don't know some of the answers to questions they may ask.

Rehearsed: This particular presentation and discussion is important, so I will have run through it a number of times before entering the room.

Respectful: The people I am meeting know their own jobs much better than I do. They don't expect me to be an expert in their business, but to see whether we can work together. I am ready to listen.

A positive mindset: I am looking forward to the meeting and, in my head, I am framing it in a positive way. I can visualise it going well, with a spirited and at times fun discussion. I can imagine high levels of rapport.

My life does not depend on this: Don't get me wrong, I want the session to go well and to win the contract on offer for our business. But I am not desperate for their work. There are many reasons why companies award contracts, some of them random, as we have discovered. I think a procurement team can sense desperation from several paces. I once met an Australian consultant called Justin who had been so successful that he no longer needed to work. He described how a potential new client phoned him one day to ask him to pitch for new business. Here is the essence of the conversation:

Client: 'We would love you to come in and talk to us about some top team development.'
Justin: 'I would love to, but please be aware my fee for the work will be $2,500.'
Client: 'Sorry, you don't understand. We are comparing several other consultants and we don't normally pay for time spent pitching for the work.'
Justin: 'You have no doubt done your research and have found some great people who will do a fine job. So, while I thank you for the invite, I will refuse your kind offer and will probably spend the day fishing instead.'
Client: 'But we really want you to do the work...'
Justin: 'Then the first meeting will cost $2,500.'

Perhaps an extreme example (but a genuine one). If there is a scale with the word 'desperate' at one end and 'indifferent' at the other, Justin was definitely towards the indifferent end. Incidentally, I did worry that his love of fishing and willingness to use this as a way to progress conversations may make him seem 'not bothered'. But the point here is that desperation is not going to feel like presence or gravitas.

Ready to challenge: I remember one of my first encounters with my own chief executive not long after I had been appointed. He called me in to see him and had some well-prepared and perhaps well-rehearsed questions for me. In my first meeting, I stood my ground and challenged him back, and in that moment I am pretty sure I gained his respect. There is a danger in many meetings that your desire to please others and meet them on their territory means that you suppress your own views. When I walk into a room full of senior people, I am ready to challenge them. I worry that too many consultants try to please the people in the room by agreeing with everything. They think this makes them seem likeable. There is, of course, another phrase for this, which is 'sucking up'. Most people spot this a mile away.

Positive self-talk: I will spend a few minutes before the meeting getting my head around the positive outcomes I want to see. I will practise the legend-building technique. I won't sit in reception with any negative thoughts or worries about the meeting. I make sure my mindset is positive.

Chapter Summary

1. Your level of self-belief in the role is critical. It fuels your expectations, actions and results.
2. You have the capacity to put on a brave face during challenges and adversity. Over time this can convert to genuine confidence.
3. Your self-talk is the most powerful voice you will hear. Suppress any inner demons intent on undermining your credibility.
4. Develop a growth mindset and see failure as a learning experience. Nothing great has been achieved without problems along the way.

CONCLUSION

I started this book by defining executive presence as building authentic credibility at the most senior levels in an organisation. In these chapters I have aimed to summarise many of the themes, ideas and practical suggestions that will help to achieve this.

I do recognise there is no such thing as a typical organisation, and the role of senior leader varies tremendously. But my intention is to present the recurring themes and issues for you to consider and reflect upon.

I thought I would conclude with a bite-size checklist of the twenty key points contained and expanded upon in these pages.

1. Think about the reputation you wish to build and get this clear in your mind.
2. You shape a reputation one day at a time, one meeting at a time, and with every interaction.
3. People make quick judgements about you, so work on your personal impact.
4. What you wear matters more than most people realise.
5. Take your cues about what to wear from the most senior people in the organisation.
6. Treat others with respect and see them as equals.
7. Practise your listening. You should use networking as a platform for you to learn more rather than sell your news or ideas.
8. Surround yourself with brilliant people. The more senior you become, the more you rely on the work and contribution of others. Your direct reports and your wider team need to be the very best they can be.
9. Create an environment in which it feels safe to have authentic discussions and where it is safe to say what is on your mind.

10. Be prepared to be challenging and ask the difficult questions.
11. Spend time thinking about and discussing the future of your department, team or function.
12. Clarity matters. The reports you draft and the presentations you prepare are all important, and they represent you and your thinking.
13. Stay calm and in control, and don't allow strong, negative emotions to be observed by others.
14. Remember that becoming more senior requires a shift in perspective. You need to take a wider, more systemic view of the organisation. You are now running the organisation, not a part of it.
15. Bring your energy and passion to work.
16. People pay a lot of attention to senior people. So take that role model responsibility seriously and project a positive image to others.
17. Work on your self-talk. The voices in your head are often more important than the ones that come out of your mouth.
18. Build your resilience. Not every day will be great and you will encounter tough times. So make sure you look after your own well-being through the pressure and chaos that leadership brings.
19. Be sensitive to other people's self-esteem. Work with them, not against them.
20. Be accountable. Pick up the challenge, accept responsibility and don't wait for others to take action.

There is no doubt that the territory of senior leadership is vague and uncertain. No coaching from me can influence the turbulence of the market place or the dynamics of change in your organisation. But I do believe profoundly that the best people to lead a team through these challenges are the people who carry themselves with executive presence as I have defined it in these pages. Pay attention to yourself; get yourself in order; be strong, calm and credible; and you are ready to face the world as a role model and leader.

Good luck with it.

Get in touch

It would be great to hear your comments, thoughts or questions. Do drop me a line to andy@development-training.com.

If you are looking for coaching or development in any of the areas discussed, get in touch or visit our website at www.development-training.com.

I love using pictures and diagrams to illustrate concepts and ideas and you will find many in this book. I am obviously constrained by the page size in presenting them here. By all means send me an email and I will forward a document with them all a lot bigger and, in some cases, more colourful.

Thanks

A few words of thanks...

Many of the ideas and models in this book were developed over time working with Ann Akers, whose reputation as a business leader and executive coach deserves the highest praise. Without her input, ideas and wisdom, this book would not exist.

Thanks to Jon Godwin from the FCA for helping with the observations on diversity and inclusion.

Thanks to all the coaching clients and business leaders I have worked with over the last fifteen years. The time we have spent together has helped shape these pages.

Thanks to all my colleagues at DTC. Our many discussions and debates have inevitably been distilled into the ideas contained in this book.

Thanks to Bryony Sutherland for being a most amazing editor.

Thanks to Caroline Goldsmith for her support in design and typesetting.

About the Author - Andy Matheson

Andy has been consulting and coaching for twenty years. He has worked with executives and senior leaders from across a wide spectrum of organisation sectors, and spends his time either coaching one-to-one or working with teams on strategy and change. He also runs programmes on executive coaching and leadership development.

He is the author of the novel Twelve Essays In Love, which was published in 2018 and is available on Amazon.

He has been involved in a number of musical projects, including the albums, Walking In Slow Motion and Essays in Love, the accompanying soundtrack to his novel. Both albums are available on Amazon and iTunes.

If you have enjoyed this book, please leave a review on Amazon. Thank you!

Printed in Great Britain
by Amazon